Arnd Plagge

Public Policy for Venture Capital

WIRTSCHAFTSWISSENSCHAFT

Arnd Plagge

Public Policy for Venture Capital

A Comparison of the United States and Germany

With a Foreword by Prof. Dr. Carl-Ludwig Holtfrerich

Deutscher Universitäts-Verlag

Bibliografische Information Der Deutschen Bibliothek
Die Deutsche Bibliothek verzeichnet diese Publikation in der Deutschen Nationalbibliografie; detaillierte bibliografische Daten sind im Internet über <http://dnb.ddb.de> abrufbar.

1. Auflage Januar 2006

Lektorat: Ute Wrasmann / Anita Wilke

Der Deutsche Universitäts-Verlag ist ein Unternehmen von Springer Science+Business Media.
www.duv.de

Umschlaggestaltung: Regine Zimmer, Dipl.-Designerin, Frankfurt/Main
Druck und Buchbinder: Rosch-Buch, Scheßlitz
Gedruckt auf säurefreiem und chlorfrei gebleichtem Papier
Printed in Germany

ISBN 3-8350-0217-1

Foreword

In view of Germany's lackluster economic performance during the 1990s, i.e., at a time when the American economy was booming, a relative lack of venture capital vis-à-vis the United States was lamented in Germany. German government programs meant to help raise venture capital in order to finance "predominantly young, technologically innovative, unlisted small- and medium-sized enterprises which, despite low current profitability, are considered to have a sufficiently large growth potential," (Deutsche Bundesbank) were to a large extent unsuccessful since their inception in the 1960s. It is well-known that Germans tend to be more risk-averse than Americans, and it is therefore no wonder that the author of this book, Arnd Plagge, finds that Germany's venture capital market is relatively underdeveloped when compared to its counterpart in the United States.

There can be no doubt that due to its investment focus on innovative start-up companies, venture capital can play an important role in fostering economic growth and the creation of modern high-skill jobs, especially by spurring the development of entirely new industries and products from such diverse and dynamic realms as pharmaceuticals, biotechnology as well as information and communication technology.

Arnd Plagge's sharp quantitative analysis of the role of venture capital and of government programs to promote it, in both Germany and the United States, is well founded theoretically and supplies empirical evidence on both countries abundantly while at the same time demonstrating how international comparisons can lead to new insights. It finds, for instance, that the venture capital market in the United States has reached a self-sustaining size and that it—in contrast to the German one—does not need much government help.

For Germany, the author comes up with a totally surprising result. Not the supply of venture capital, which German government programs try to promote mainly through subsidized loans with low interest rates, is the bottleneck for the growth of this market. Rather, the demand for venture capital is wanting in Germany, as evidenced by the fact that the already available pool of such capital is largely not being disbursed. Arnd Plagge concludes that the German government would be well-advised to abandon its efforts to promote the supply of venture capital and instead to begin directing its programs at the demand side of this market.

This main result of an academic study bears an extremely important message for policy makers, which for the benefit of the German economy, the future living standard of Germany's citizens, and their own record of performance they should not ignore.

Carl-Ludwig Holtfrerich
Professor of Economics at the Freie Universität Berlin
John F. Kennedy Institute for North American Studies

Preface

I began my work on venture capital in the U.S. and Germany sometime in the year 2000, i.e., at the height of the Internet bubble, and unlike the stock market, my interest in the subject has never again declined. Indeed, even though the results of my research are now available in the form of this book—which is the culmination of research and writing that lasted several years—I certainly do not consider it the last word on the subject and hope that more research on venture capital and public policies aimed at it will be published in the future.

While writing this book, I incurred many debts, and I would like to thank those who helped and guided me along the way. My earliest work on venture capital was for a term paper I wrote under the supervision of Welf Werner at the Freie Universität Berlin's John F. Kennedy Institute for North American Studies. Welf later also served on the committee that evaluated my master's thesis on venture capital, and I thank him for his guidance and the interest he showed.

A large part of my data collection efforts took place at the University of Virginia while I was a visiting student there in the academic year 2001/02. Special thanks go to Paolo Ramezzana, who agreed without hesitation to serve as my supervisor for a rather preliminary research project "on venture capital," and to Gordon M. Stewart, who was my academic mentor while I was visiting UVa. I also gratefully acknowledge the support of the DAAD, without whose scholarship I would not have been able to spend two semesters in Charlottesville.

The next stage of my research again took place at the Freie Universität Berlin, where I started to write my master's thesis on "Public Policy for Venture Capital in the U.S. and Germany" in mid-2003. I finished the work in November 2003, at a time when I had already returned to the U.S. for graduate studies at the University of Rochester. Also in 2003, I worked as a research assistant for Caroline Fohlin, whose incisive questions on the venture capital markets in the U.S. and Germany helped sharpen the argument presented in this book considerably.

The final impetus that ultimately led to the publication of this book came from the Kennedy Institute's Carl-Ludwig Holtfrerich, who was the main advisor for my master's thesis and whose positive feedback prompted me to pursue the topic further. His constant encouragement to turn my thesis into a book led me to update and extend it considerably during the summer of 2005. At this stage, I especially benefitted from access to the archives of the German private equity and venture capital association, which was generously provided by the BVK's Attila Dahmann.

Last but not least, special thanks go to my parents, Gertrud and Josef Plagge, who have always supported me—both morally and financially—and still continue to do so.

Arnd Plagge

Contents

List of figures

List of tables

List of abbreviations

ACF	autocorrelation function
ADF	Augmented Dickey-Fuller
AIC	Akaike information criterion
AIM	Alternative Investment Market
ARD	American Research & Development
ARIMA	autoregessive integrated moving average
BJTU	Beteiligungskapital für junge Technologieunternehmen
BTU	Beteiligungskapital für kleine Technologieunternehmen
BVK	Bundesverband deutscher Kapitalbeteiligungsgesellschaften e.V.
	German private equity and venture capital association
CEO	chief executive officer
DAX	Deutscher Aktienindex
DEC	Digital Equipment Corporation
DtA	Deutsche Ausgleichsbank
DM	Deutsche Mark
EIF	European Investment Fund
ERISA	Employee Retirement Income Security Act of 1974
ERP	European Recovery Program
EVCA	European Venture Capital Association
HCCM	heteroscedasticity-consistent covariance matrix
GDP	gross domestic product
IPO	initial public offering
KBG	Kapitalbeteiligungsgesellschaft

KfW	Kreditanstalt für Wiederaufbau
LBO	leveraged buy-out
MBI	management buy-in
MBO	management buy-out
na	not available
NASDAQ	National Association of Security Dealers Automated Quotation
NPV	net present value
NVCA	National Venture Capital Association
OECD	Organisation for Economic Co-operation and Development
OLS	ordinary least-squares
PACF	partial autocorrelation function
PEMC	public equity market capitalization
R&D	research and development
ROI	return on investment
SBA	Small Business Administration
SBIC	Small Business Investment Company
SBIR	Small Business Innovation Research
SME	small and medium-sized enterprises
S&P	Standard & Poor's
tbg	Technologie-Beteiligungsgesellschaft
TOU	Programm zur Förderung technologieorientierter Unternehmensgründungen
UK	United Kingdom
U.S.	United States of America
USD	United States dollars
VC	venture capital
VCs	venture capitalists
WFG	Deutsche Wagnisfinanzierungs-Gesellschaft mbH

Note: 1 billion = 1,000 million.

Exchange rate used: € 1 = DM 1.95583.

Chapter 1

The nature and role of venture capital

Venture capital has become an important engine of economic growth in the United States over the last decades. For instance, Gompers and Lerner (2001a: 83) state: "No matter how we look at the numbers, venture capital activity clearly serves as an important source for economic development, wealth and job creation, and innovation." Gilson (2002: 2) likewise asserts:

> "The venture capital market and firms whose creation and early stages were financed by venture capital are among the crown jewels of the American economy. Beyond representing an important engine of macroeconomic growth and job creation, these firms have been a major force in commercializing cutting edge science, whether through their impact on existing industries as with the radical changes in pharmaceuticals catalyzed by venture-backed firms' commercialization of biotechnology, or by their role in developing entirely new industries as with the emergence of the internet and world wide web."

It is no wonder, then, that other countries try to foster their own venture capital industries, often via extensive public programs. Germany is no exception to this rule, and the first aim of this book is to evaluate public policy programs meant to strengthen the venture capital sector in Germany. The second, closely related goal is to make data on the German venture capital market readily available to an English-speaking audience. Special care has been taken to offer a thorough overview of what is known about the overall German market. In addition to numerous references to the existing literature, most of the data in this book has been compiled from primary sources. Maybe most importantly, a novel and very comprehensive side-by-side quantitative comparison of the American and German venture capital markets is presented in chapters 5 and 6.

The main finding of this book is that the prevalent German public policy of targeting the supply of venture capital is misguided and will not lead to more vibrant venture capital activity. A thorough review of the relevant theory and the available empirical evidence reveals that while a strong case can be made in favor of public intervention, the main schemes meant to help expand the venture capital market in Germany that are now in place are ill-designed. Only a drastic reversal of priorities will lead to the desired outcome of a more active German venture capital market and in turn higher economic growth.

Before discussing the intricacies of the market in the U.S. and Germany and turning to how venture capital activity can potentially be influenced, we first have to clarify what exactly venture capital is and how it functions. The remainder of this chapter thus sets out to provide a concise introduction to venture capital for readers who are so far unfamiliar with the industry. Having explained what venture capital is and how it works in section 1.1 and 1.2, section 1.3 provides a roadmap for the remainder of this book.[1]

[1]No attention at all is paid here to the business administration literature on how venture capital firms work. For an introduction to these topics, see the surveys by Gorman and Sahlman (1989), Lerner (2000), and Sahlman (1990) for the U.S. and Schefczyk (1998), Wupperfeld (1996), and Zemke (1995) for Germany.

1.1 Definitions

So far, in the literature there is no coherent definition of the term "venture capital." For example, Wright and Robbie (1998: 521) define it as follows: "Venture capital is typically defined as the investment by professional investors of long-term, unquoted, risk equity finance in new firms where the primary reward is an eventual capital gain, supplemented by dividend yield." A more precise definition is given in Deutsche Bundesbank (2000: 16):

> "In the narrower sense, venture capital denotes equity holdings in predominantly young, technologically innovative, unlisted small and medium-sized enterprises which, despite low current profitability, are considered to have a sufficiently large growth potential. [...] Venture capital investment companies provide the young firms not only with equity capital but also with extensive management expertise and other advisory services."

As is already evident from these two examples, a common denominator for the scope and exact meaning of the term "venture capital" does not exist.[2] I therefore use the following characterization:

> *Venture capital* is additional equity finance provided by independent third parties to finance early-stage operations and is intended to remain in a given not publicly traded company for a limited time. It also includes the provision of management assistance.[3]

This definition of the term venture capital is basically identical to the American concept of venture capital. The broader notion of venture capital

[2] However, excellent overviews of the U.S. private equity industry do exist; see for instance Fenn et al. (1995). Also, outstanding relatively concise overviews of the literature on venture capital and private equity can be found in Mason and Harrison (1999), Gompers and Lerner (2001b), and Wright and Robbie (1998).

[3] Note that this definition excludes the so-called corporate venture capital funds, as they are by definition not independent. For good overviews of this form of start-up financing, see Chesbrough (2002), Hellmann (2002), Gompers and Lerner (1998b), McNally (1997), and Sykes (1990).

prevalent in Europe, which includes along with early-stage financing later-stage investment activity such as management and leveraged buyouts, as well, will subsequently be referred to as private equity:

> *Private equity* subsumes all forms of venture capital plus all capital that constitutes additional equity finance provided by third parties to finance later-stage operations and that is intended to remain in a given not publicly traded company for a limited time.

Early-stage financing, in turn, spans three phases: seed financing, start-up financing, and expansion-stage financing. All three stages have in common that the investments made here are meant to help grow the business: They go either into expense investments (e.g., manufacturing, marketing) or into the balance sheet (providing fixed assets and working capital).[4] In this book, only early-stage financing will be referred to as venture capital.

Later-stage financing, in contrast, can be subdivided into bridge or mezzanine financing, the buy-out sector with management buy-outs, management buy-ins, and leveraged buy-outs, as well as into specific forms of refinancing of distressed debt and turnaround financing. Investments at a later-stage level are not primarily aimed at growing the business, but often fill a void where other forms of financing are not readily available from other outside investors, who shy away from the above average risks associated with investments like turnaround financing. In this book, later-stage investments will be referred to as belonging to the category of private equity investments.

The purpose of venture capital financing can thus largely be derived from its definition. Venture capital often constitutes the only possibility for a young start-up firm to finance its ideas and work on its products until they are introduced in the market. Especially young companies from high-tech and other related areas often have a promising business idea that suggests a sufficiently large market potential, but the financing of the first steps often proves to be extremely challenging, as no or little collateral is available in such cases.

[4] Zider (1998: 132)

Apart from the possibility that the company's founders pay the costs incurred in the beginning out of their own pockets, they can essentially take three other forms of financing into consideration. The first is to take a loan out of the bank, the second one turning to wealthy individuals known as "business angels" for outside financing, and the third the reliance on venture capital. While the first possibility cannot be ruled out altogether, nearly all start-ups lack the (physical) assets which are necessary to secure a loan. Working with a business angel might prove viable in the very beginning, but as a company's financing needs increase, the resources of these market participants are often quickly exhausted.[5] Additionally, only venture capital financing can generally be regarded as an infusion of "smart money," meaning that venture capitalists will provide management assistance to their portfolio companies. The latter aspect also defines the nature of venture capital – it is much more than just money given by a passive investor. Once a venture capitalist decides to fund a project, she will become actively involved in the portfolio company, too. When looking at what venture capitalists do, it is therefore often most useful to compare their work to consulting firms rather than banks to understand what makes them special.

Unfortunately, this central aspect of venture capital is often overlooked in the literature, and it is no wonder then that several articles try to directly compare venture capital firms with banks.[6] Those closely involved in the process, on the other hand, seem to have a keen sense of what distinguishes venture capitalists from banks and other traditional financial intermediaries, as the following excerpt from a book on serial entrepreneur Jim Clark, founder of Silicon Graphics, Netscape, and Healtheon – i.e., someone with ample first-hand experience with the U.S. venture capital industry – makes clear:

[5] By now, there is a large body of literature on "angel financing." See for instance Benjamin and Sandles (1998), Lerner (1998), Mason and Harrison (1996), and Steier and Greenwood (2000). For a country-specific study for the U.S. see Sohl (2003); for Germany, see Brettel (2002) and Cadenhead et al. (2000).

[6] See for example Dietz (2002), Landier (2001), and Ueda (undated).

> "Until that moment of high despair in early 1997, it was never entirely clear why Clark had gone to the venture capitalists on Sand Hill Road in the first place. He didn't need their money. He had more money than all of them combined. But he did, after all, need them: he needed them to translate his extraordinary ambition into the ordinary language understood by corporate America. The man who groped for the new new thing was in many ways ill suited for mainstream business. Clark knew that the time would come to put a smiley corporate face on his ferocious ambition. He knew, also, that he did not know how to do this. [...]
>
> The venture capitalists, on the other hand, talked the talk and walked the walk. In tone and spirit they were not all that different from Serious American Executives. The VCs had been to business school, they spoke the jargon, they wore the suits, or at least owned them. [...] One VC in particular had a gift for persuading mainstream CEOs that the only place to be was a Silicon Valley start-up: John Doerr. [...] [Clark] asked Doerr to join Healtheon's board and to help him recruit a CEO."[7]

It is also important to stress what exactly is meant by supply of and demand for venture capital in the context of this book. *Supply of venture capital* refers to how much money investors are willing to give to venture capitalists. In contrast to this straightforward definition of supply, demand is more difficult to define. One important concept to keep in mind here is that of the so-called "hurdle rate." This rate, which can be interpreted as the interest a venture capital firm expects to earn on an investment, is exogenously given. As venture capital investments in equilibrium must be as profitable as all other financial investments after adjusting for risk, the hurdle rate determines which investment proposals are acceptable to a venture capitalist in the first place. If somebody approaches a venture capital firm with a business plan that promises a return on investment (ROI) of, say, 10 percent per year, while

[7] Lewis (2000: 147-148)

the hurdle rate stands at 20 percent, then the venture capitalist will walk away from such a deal. Only when the return an entrepreneur promises to earn with her idea clears the hurdle will the venture capitalist invest. From the perspective of an entrepreneur, venture capital thus has a "price" equal to the hurdle rate. Only when a start-up firm is able to earn returns in excess of, say, 20 percent per year on the venture capital money it receives, will this count as demand for venture capital in the sense of this book. Thus, *demand for venture capital* is here understood as equivalent to qualified, i.e., clearing the hurdle rate, demand for funds.

An analogy might help clarify what demand for venture capital really means here. Imagine a car dealer offering a BMW for $50,000, which exactly equals cost. The demand for the BMW is then equal to the number of people who are willing to pay $50,000 for the car. Likewise, a venture capitalist will offer money and management assistance to interested start-ups on the condition that she receives a given price for it, which is simply equivalent to the expected annual return on her venture capital money. Thus, the sheer number of entrepreneurs submitting business plans and asking for venture capital funding does not equal demand, as this would be like asking how many people would buy the BMW for $40,000, $30,000, and so on, all the way down to unlimited demand at $0.

1.2 The venture capital cycle

The venture capital cycle constitutes the core of every venture capital investment.[8] It is made up of three stages: fundraising, investing, and divesting. All three phases play a crucial role for venture capitalists as well as their (potential) portfolio companies. In addition to the three phases, one also has to distinguish between various market participants, and figure 1.1 gives a stylized overview of the market structure within which venture capital and private equity firms in the U.S. operate.

Every venture capital investment starts with the fundraising phase. It is here that venture capitalists turn to institutional investors and wealthy individuals in order to raise money for a fund. Generally, venture capital firms are structured as venture capital limited partnerships. Such a partnership is made up of a small group of experienced managers who provide promising businesses with capital and management assistance. As the partners are paid a basic salary that depends on the size of the fund managed by them plus a bonus depending on how well their fund performs, they normally have an incentive to raise as much money as possible.

The second stage, the actual process of investing the raised funds in portfolio companies, is the most important step in the venture capital cycle. At this stage, venture capitalists look out for appropriate investments that promise a high rate of return on the invested capital, normally running between more than 100 percent in the case of seed financing to about 30 percent in the case of the later-stage bridge financing. As the risk of a total loss of the investment hovers around at least 20 percent, these high rates of possible returns are crucial to offset losses incurred by inevitable write-offs. In the end, a return of at least 20 percent per year is deemed necessary to justify the fund's existence given the high risks and very limited liquidity associated with venture capital investments.

---

[8] Gompers and Lerner's (1999) book by the same title is the standard reference on the venture capital cycle.

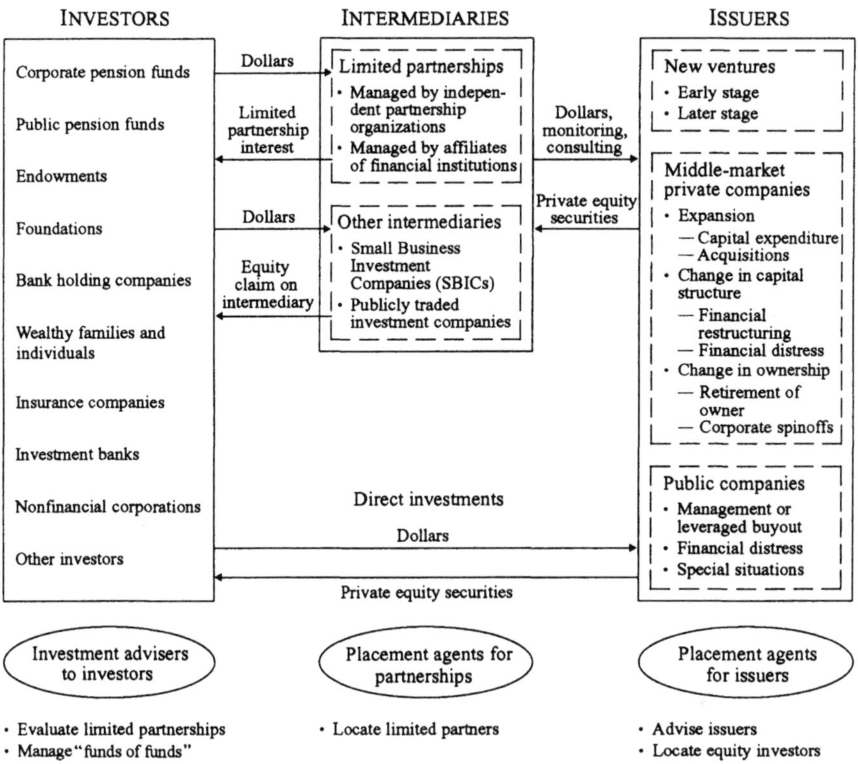

Figure 1.1
Overview of the organized private equity market in the U.S.
Source: Adapted from Fenn et al. (1995: 4, diagram 1).

In order to overcome principal-agent problems, venture capitalists have devised a series of mechanisms that are ultimately meant to help align the behavior of a portfolio company with the preferences of the venture capitalists. Typically, these devices include various forms of intensive screening (*ex ante* monitoring), a range of contractual arrangements, and close interim and *ex post* monitoring that is generally associated with equity stakeholding and board membership.[9]

[9]For good introductions to these topics, see the empirical work by Cumming (2005) and Kaplan and Strömberg' (2001) more theoretical article.

Kaplan and Strömberg (2000) have compiled a large body of empirical evidence stating that the initial screening of potential portfolio firms is a process that venture capitalists take very seriously. Once a potential portfolio company has cleared this stage, a lengthy contract between the two parties is set up. Typically, it includes a separation of cash-flow rights, voting rights, and board rights, among others. In a later study, Kaplan and Strömberg (2003) find that managers of portfolio companies that perform poorly typically lose most of their control over their firm. On the other hand, if the portfolio company does well, the venture capitalists mostly hold on to their cash-flow rights, but loosen their grip over other control rights.

In addition, venture capitalists usually stage their investments, i.e., they give money at different stages in the life cycle of a portfolio company, often once a milestone has been reached.[10] This limits the risk of losing high sums and also helps venture capitalists exert influence over their portfolio companies. Should an investment not perform as planned or should continuing arguments over a company's future direction arise, then the venture capitalists can simply turn off the supply of money and thereby potentially force the portfolio company's management team to alter its stance. Finally, as Bergemann and Hege (1998) and Lerner (1995) assert, close monitoring via board membership is an essential component of venture capitalists' activities and can add considerable value to the portfolio company.

If an investment has performed well, the venture capitalists will try to divest. To do so, they can choose between three major options: an initial public offering (IPO), a trade sale, or a buy-back. The latter is mostly restricted to later-stage financing, as the portfolio company here buys back the equity held by the venture capitalists. Generally, still relatively young high-tech companies, for example, usually lack the resources to strike such a deal. In this case, an IPO or a trade sale constitutes the normal divestment procedure. In a trade sale, the portfolio company is sold to another, normally larger company. Finally, the IPO represents the usual means to sell a formerly

[10]See Giudici and Paleari (2000), Gompers (1995), Neher (1999), Sahlman (1990), and Wang and Zhou (2004) for more detailed discussions of this point.

private company to the public by listing it on a stock exchange. In this case, the venture capitalist and those who initially provided her with funds can simply sell the shares they retained during the IPO on the stock market, typically after a so-called "lockup period" of six months has expired.

Once the three stages have been completed, the venture capital cycle can start again. Usually, as the life of most funds is limited to eight to ten years, the money from selling the portfolio companies to third parties is disbursed to the original investors, the limited partners, who can then decide whether they want to invest their money in a new fund created by the same venture capitalists or if they want to turn to another partnership that promises higher returns or if they prefer other investments altogether.

1.3 Plan of the book

In chapter 2, theoretical arguments for and against government intervention in the venture capital market are reviewed. Then, in chapters 3, on the U.S., and 4, on Germany, an extensive quantitative description of the U.S. and German venture capital markets that heavily draws on primary sources – mainly the yearly statistics published by the National Venture Capital Association (NVCA) in the U.S. and the Bundeverband deutscher Kapitalbeteiligungsgesellschaften (BVK) in Germany – follows. These chapters also provide background information on public policy initiatives aimed at the venture capital markets in both countries. In order to substantiate the claim that the German venture capital market is suffering from lack of demand, chapter 5 examines how the German venture capital market has so far performed relative to its U.S. counterpart. Chapter 6 is dedicated to a discussion of the alleged link between IPOs and venture capital fundraising activity and offers econometric evidence that it does *not* lie at the heart of the weaker performance of the German market, while Chapter 7 returns more generally to the question whether supply or demand factors play a more important role in holding back venture capital activity in Germany. Chapter 8 concludes.

Chapter 2

Theoretical perspectives on public policy for venture capital

Every work that sets out to evaluate the design and impact of government policy in the economic realm has to answer one fundamental question first, namely whether a case can be made for government intervention at all. The aim of this chapter is therefore to explain what exactly can justify government intervention in the venture capital market.[1]

The answer I provide to this question is split up into three parts. First, several empirical and theoretical studies on the firm- and industry-level impact of venture capital financing with regard to patenting, research and development (R&D) activity, and the professionalization of sponsored enterprises are reviewed. The second part employs a macroeconomic perspective and discusses insights into how modern economies grow that are based on the recent endogenous growth literature, and the central role that ideas and R&D play in such models is emphasized.

I then introduce an extension of the standard endogenous growth model to better capture the empirically observed effects which venture capital financing has on knowledge production and commercialization. Finally, market

[1] Boadway and Tremblay (2005) provide a broad overview of a closely related topic; their analysis focuses on public policies targeted at start-up entrepreneurs.

failures that in the presence of externalities and spill-overs cause an under-supply of R&D relative to the socially optimal level are first portrayed theoretically and subsequently evaluated based upon empirical results from the pertinent literature. Taken together, the three parts help establish a strong case in favor of public intervention in venture capital markets.

2.1 Parameters for model calibration

Any discussion of the impact of venture capital on economic growth has to rely on various parameters. The goal of this section is therefore to review the best available research on the empirical growth effects of venture capital financing and to extract the parameters that are needed in the models presented below from it. Unfortunately, thorough empirical studies on the impact of venture capital on inventive activity and R&D are still scarce. Nonetheless, for the U.S. there are two especially useful papers by Hellmann and Puri (2000) and Kortum and Lerner (2001) on this topic.[2]

Before we turn to a discussion of the venture capital-specific literature, it is worthwhile to quickly take a look at the larger picture. There has been a long-standing discussion about whether large or small firms are the most likely source of innovation in a market-based economy. The view that small firms are more innovative can be traced back to at least the early twentieth century, when Joseph Schumpeter put this argument forward in his book "The Theory of Economic Development."[3] More recent empirical research has not been able to provide any clear-cut answers in this area, though.[4] Yet, Henderson (1993) finds in a case study of the photolithographic alignment equipment industry that established firms tend to outperform start-ups when

[2]See also Roling (2001) for a sophisticated discussion of macro-level evidence. He uses a panel-data approach to measure the effect of venture capital on innovative activity.

[3]Schumpeter (1934[1912]). It is worth noting that Schumpeter later reversed his stance and argued in his book "Capitalism, Socialism, and Democracy" that established firms with some monopoly power were better suited to drive innovative activity, not least because they were able to appropriate ideas from smaller companies and subsequently make use of economies of scale; see Schumpeter (1942).

[4]See for example the comprehensive study by Baldwin and Scott (1987).

it comes to incremental innovation, while new entrants are more successful in pursuing radical innovation. On balance, then, both large, established firms and start-ups are sources of innovation in an economy, even though they tend to cover different segments of the market for ideas.[5] As will soon become clear, venture capital-backed start-ups, in turn, tend to outperform both their non-venture capital-backed start-up peers and large corporations in terms of innovative efficiency.

In a seminal paper, Hellmann and Puri (2000) use a sample of 173 Silicon Valley start-ups from the technology sector to study the impact of venture capital financing on product market outcomes. One-third of their sample consists of firms that never received venture backing and thus functions as the control group against which the impact of venture capital financing is benchmarked. After extensively controlling for selection effects and reverse causation, they find that venture capital-backed companies are often innovators in their field and that these firms in particular witness a significant reduction in the time it takes to bring a product to market. Moreover, this effect remains sizable in the case of venture capital-backed imitators, albeit on a smaller scale.

Kortum and Lerner (2001) examine a large dataset of U.S. patents issued to U.S. inventors that was compiled by the U.S. Patent and Trademark Office, consisting of yearly observations for twenty manufacturing industries for the years 1965 to 1992. After controlling for a whole array of potential distortions, they find that venture capital financing has a significant impact on patenting rates. According to their estimates, venture capital-backed R&D outpaces the efficiency of traditional corporate R&D efforts by a factor of 3.1 when averaging across their preferred regressions. Interestingly, they also conclude that "by 1998 venture funding accounted for about 14% of U.S. innovative activity."[6]

[5] Gans et al. (2002) provide some further thoughts on this issue.
[6] Kortum and Lerner (2001: 28)

Similarly, the OECD investigated the link between innovation and venture capital in a 1996 study. This extensive inquiry, covering many OECD member countries, sees a strong link between venture capital investments and the efficiency of R&D, which is described as follows: "Professional skills and techniques used in the screening, selection and management of R&D and innovation projects have become more sophisticated and demonstrated remarkable progress. This is true in both the case of large organizations' *project management* techniques, and the steering of small/entrepreneurial projects by *venture-capitalists* and other investors."[7]

In a follow-up paper to their 2000 article, Hellmann and Puri (2002) also find evidence that receiving venture capital-backing results in a professionalization of the start-ups' management, including better human resource policies, the adoption of stock option plans, and the hiring of outsiders such as marketing vice presidents and, notably, often also new CEOs.[8] The view that venture capitalists not only invest in "winners" to start with, but also help build them, is echoed in Baum and Silverman (2004), who assert for a cross-panel of biotechnology firms: "Specifically, we find that VCs are attracted to firms that have technology that can lead to strong future performance but that are teetering on the edge of short-term failure. This pattern suggests that VCs select startups for funding based on a combined logic of 'scouting' out strong technology (and relationships) and 'coaching' via the injection of management skill."[9]

Finally, Keuschnigg (2004) makes a first effort to base the empirical observations presented in the preceding paragraphs on theoretical microfoundations in the context of a general equilibrium analysis. He concludes: "Innovation results from the joint efforts of both entrepreneurs and informed financiers. While the entrepreneur contributes the key technological idea in starting up a new firm, the VC supports the firm with managerial advice

[7]OECD (1996: 20, emphasis in original)

[8]Relatedly, Davila et al. (2003) find empirical evidence for the notion that a company that has received venture capital-backing can credibly signal its quality to other potential employees, too.

[9]Baum and Silverman (2003: 431-432)

which draws on her extensive business experience and industry knowledge. [...] It was shown how important structural parameters of the VC industry, such as the experience and market knowledge of VCs, determine the growth rate."[10]

What all these studies make clear is that venture capitalists indeed do offer useful services to their portfolio companies and thus add value beyond what other financial intermediaries, such as a bank extending a loan, would typically be able to provide.[11]

Yet, one question that quickly arises in this context is why not more R&D efforts are carried out by independent firms with venture capital-backing, given that these seem to be considerably more efficient than similar run-of-the-mill corporate R&D initiatives. Again, the literature in this area is still in its infancy, but Anand and Galetovic (2000b) provide an excellent starting point for thinking about this issue.[12] They develop a model with two potential investors, a venture capitalist and a corporation, and study how the sequence of financing R&D activities varies given different property rights setups. One key assumption is that the fruits of the research efforts become embodied in the researcher, and she can walk away with the results after the research and before the development phase. Depending on whether property rights are weak or strong, meaning that the probability that the original financier can establish its rights over the innovation's cash flow should the researcher decide to switch financiers once the research phase has come to an end is low or high, different outcomes follow:

[10] Keuschnigg (2004: 258)

[11] It should be noted, however, that some papers reach deviating conclusions. See for example the theoretical discussion by Ueda (2002) and the empirical paper by Wang et al. (2003).

[12] For further reading on this issue, consult the references given in Anand and Galetovic (2000b). See also Hellmann (1998) for a discussion of how potential hold-up by entrepreneurs influences the venture capital financing process, and Anand and Galetovic (2000a) for an overview of how property rights over information influence market behavior and the regional structure of the venture capital and other financial industries.

> "While we assumed that VC- and corporate-financed research were equally efficient, our results suggest that self-selection of researchers may lead VCs to finance higher-quality projects. In our model, more profitable projects attract VCs because they can commit to a surplus-sharing rule, while the corporation cannot. [...] We have shown here that joint activities may also facilitate corporate R&D finance. For example, local spillovers and strong product-market competition from the corporation enlarge the scope of corporate R&D finance when property rights are weak. More generally, corporations exist because doing many activities facilitates the exploitation of economies of scope and complementarities, which are absent in standalone projects. This suggests that corporations may *optimally* sacrifice incentives to exploit complementarities."[13]

Following this logic, while existing venture capital-backed R&D initiatives are remarkably more efficient than their corporate counterparts, most R&D projects simply cannot be carried out efficiently by small start-ups. One is faced with a classic self-selection mechanism here, which should warn us against inferring based on the observed projects that large corporations are always less efficient when carrying out R&D projects than venture capital-backed firms.

One last paper deserves mentioning in this context, too. Huang and Xu (2003) observe that even large corporations with sufficient funds to finance a given research project regularly resort to syndication with a venture capitalist. They attribute this behavior to the difficulty of large firms to make a credible commitment to terminate an unsuccessful R&D project timely. Unlike in the largely antagonistic setups discussed above, in this case corporations and venture capitalists form a symbiotic relationship that leads to optimal outcomes for both.

[13] Anand and Galetovic (2000b: 640-641, emphasis in original)

2.2 Adapted endogenous growth model

As the aforementioned empirical studies suggest, venture capital-backed firms on average tend to file more patent applications than otherwise comparable companies. In order to capture this fact on a more general theoretical level, in the following I modify a standard endogenous growth model found in many textbooks, which is often simply referred to by the name Romer model, called this way after its originator Paul Romer.[14] Before doing so, however, the main elements of the standard model as presented in Jones (2002) are quickly reviewed.[15]

It should be stressed that two terms, which take center stage when discussing endogenous growth models, are used in what follows in ways that might be unfamiliar to some, so it is worth giving their exact definition. "*Technology* is the way inputs to the production process are transformed into output. [...] *Ideas* improve the technology of production. A new idea allows a given bundle of inputs to produce more or better output."[16]

The basic notation for a simple endogenous growth production function in turn is:

$$Y = K^{\alpha}(AL_Y)^{1-\alpha} \tag{2.1}$$

In this equation, Y denotes GDP, K the capital stock, L_Y labor, and A the stock of ideas. For the moment, let α be a parameter between 0 and 1 that we do not have to analyze further.

Compared to the standard neoclassical growth model, growth in A is not determined exogenously in this case, but rather endogenized. As the rationale behind extending the Romer model in our case is to incorporate the effect venture capital exerts on the economy's growth rate via higher patenting and overall more efficient R&D activity, we have to delve a little deeper into the intricacies of the model to see how new ideas themselves are produced.

14 Cf. Romer (1986, 1990, 1994).

15 The exposition and notation here closely follows the one in Jones (2002: 97-123).

16 Jones (2002: 79, emphasis in original)

In the simplest case, if we let $\dot{A}$ denote the number of ideas produced in a given moment, L_A the number of people engaged in research, and $\bar{\delta}$ the rate at which new ideas are discovered, we arrive at the following equation for $\dot{A}$:

$$\dot{A} = \bar{\delta} L_A \tag{2.2}$$

Based upon the empirical observation that venture capital-backed research is more efficient than research in a corporate setting when it comes to further development and commercialization, I augment the standard Romer model and introduce a factor μ to account for this fact. Let L_{VC} denote the fraction of researchers in venture capital-backed projects and θ be the factor by which these people are more efficient at commercialization. Define μ as:

$$\mu = \theta L_{VC} \tag{2.3}$$

In other words, not simply the rate $\bar{\delta}$ at which ideas are discovered matters, but also the rate at which these discoveries are subsequently used plays a role. We obtain a new identity for the venture capital-backed stock of ideas, $\dot{A}_{VC}$:

$$\dot{A}_{VC} = \bar{\delta}(L_A + \mu) \tag{2.4}$$

If we take this extension seriously, it is immediately clear that a larger venture capital-backed sector leads to higher growth for the economy. For convenience of computation, this setup in effect counts the researchers in venture capital-backed areas multiple times, once as part of L_A, and then again, according to how many times more effective they are, in μ. For example, if they are three times as effective as their counterparts in the traditional corporate sector, as the empirical results by Kortum and Lerner (2001) suggest, then the work of every "venture capital researcher" is counted as if she were three researchers in the corporate sector at the same time.

Altogether, this is admittedly a very simple extension of the widely used Romer model, but it points to a way for explaining why the growth rates in the U.S. and Germany, for example, differed notably in the late 1990s, something that more traditional endogenous growth models with their sole focus on the world technological frontier cannot account for.[17]

It would be misleading to assume that a shift towards more venture capital-backed R&D would lead to permanently higher growth rates, however. As is regularly pointed out in the literature on endogenous growth, a permanent increase of the population devoted to finding ideas affects the growth rate along a transition path to a new steady state, altering only the level of technology and thus income, but not long-run growth rates.[18] The same holds for increased efficiency of commercialization — in the very long run, the growth rate of the number of researchers in venture capital-backed sectors cannot be higher than the growth rate of those employed in other research areas, as otherwise the former would at some point exceed the total number of researchers, which is impossible.

Depending on the value of θ, these so-called transition dynamics can have a very long half-life, though. For a similar setup, Jones (1995; 776, table 1) calculates that these effects can last for 62 to 674 years, depending on the values chosen for the relevant variables and assuming that the growth rate of the economy is 2 percent in the steady state, which is a reasonable approximation for both the U.S. and Germany.

Despite these caveats, though, it is clear that a vigorous venture capital-backed sector can lead to higher GDP even when the overall input of labor and capital is held constant in equation 2.1. Thus, in addition to the microlevel effects described above, one can also establish a good theoretical case in favor of a vibrant venture capital sector at the macroeconomic level.

---

[17] See Aghion and Howitt (1998) and Jones (2002) for an extensive treatment of these and many other issues related to endogenous growth. Jones (1999) provides a more succinct overview of the main issues.

[18] For more details, see the articles by Howitt (2000), Jones (1995), Segerstrom (1998), and Young (1998).

2.3 Market failures in R&D

One additional observation follows more or less directly from the preceding discussion of the Romer model. Generally, overall R&D expenditures in an economy are too low. If one looks even deeper into the model than the last paragraphs do, one stumbles upon three externalities that are intimately connected with R&D efforts.[19] The first arises in the form of a knowledge spillover: to the extent that knowledge cannot be kept secret, others can profit from new ideas without having to pay the inventor for her efforts. One prominent example is the invention of calculus, which has proven invaluable to many researchers, yet these never accordingly compensated its inventors.

The second positive externality is the consumer-surplus effect, meaning that even if an idea generates monopoly profits, consumers capture a fraction of the total value, the consumer surplus; only in the case of perfect price discrimination would this not be true. Finally, the third externality works in the other direction. It may simply be that more than one person is working on a given idea, and this duplication of research effort lowers overall social welfare. It turns out, however, that the first two externalities empirically easily outweigh the last one.

The externalities connected to R&D ultimately justify public intervention in the market and thus in the venture capital sector. One question that has remained unanswered so far is why the often handsome higher returns to venture capital-backed research do not suffice to induce private actors to invest in this market segment at the optimal level. The answer lies buried in the endogenous growth model: As no firm can completely internalize the social returns to its R&D efforts, there is an undersupply of such efforts, or, in other words, we face a classic market failure here.

Simply trusting that the market will respond to the fact that venture capital-backed research is more efficient will thus not suffice to induce the socially optimal level of such efforts. Even though to my knowledge no one

[19] The interested reader should consult Jones (2002: 98-123) for an extensive discussion of this issue.

has yet estimated the socially optimal level of venture capital activity in an economy, a look at the existing literature on social returns to R&D in general proves instructive.

In a seminal paper, Jones and Williams (1998) introduce an elaborate model to estimate the social returns to R&D and connect their findings to the empirical productivity literature. This finally leads them to assert that "a conservative estimate indicates that optimal investment in research is more than two to four times actual investment," suggesting major market failure and thereby a large potential role for public policy in this area.[20]

Klette et al. (2000) revise five studies that try to directly evaluate the social returns from subsidies to commercial R&D activities and find that in four cases at least the performance of the directly targeted firms increased. However, they also point to the need for more comprehensive studies that take spillover effects to other firms into account.

In a recent study, Link et al. (2002) pursue just such an approach and assert that their "results suggest that the establishment of the [United States'] Commerce Department's Advanced Technology Program, which provides financial support to firms that engage in collaborative research projects, induced firms to engage in additional (privately financed) RJVs [research joint ventures]. This is a spillover mechanism that warrants further attention as national innovation systems evolve."[21]

If we accept the proposition that R&D levels are generally too low, the question arises whether public intervention can induce a shift to another equilibrium. In their survey of the pertinent literature, David et al. (2000) ask whether public R&D spending can be seen as complementary to private R&D spending or if it just substitutes for and tends to crowd out private R&D. Interestingly, no clear-cut answer emerges from their review of the econometric evidence accumulated from the mid-1960s on. Indeed, they report that 11 out of 33 studies overall report a "net" substitution of private R&D efforts

[20] Jones and Williams (1998: 1134)

[21] Link et al. (2002: 1459); see also Chang et al. (2002)'s paper on the Advanced Technology Program.

by public ones. Yet, even though the literature is still inconclusive, the fact remains that two thirds of the studies that David et al. (2000) review do not report a net substitution, lending credence to the notion that attaining a higher equilibrium is indeed possible.[22]

Wallsten (2000), in stark contrast, finds for a sample of firms participating in the U.S.' Small Business Innovation Research (SBIR) program that public R&D grants awarded to them "crowd out firm-financed R&D dollar for dollar."[23] This at least lends some credibility to the view that government programs that are meant to mitigate market failures often create incentives for the private sector that run counter to those good intentions.[24]

One further observation deserves attention. As Martin and Scott (2000) convincingly argue, no single approach will be optimal for all modes of innovation. This is an important point to keep in mind when one tries to answer the question what a venture capital market can realistically be expected to achieve in the R&D realm and for the economy in general. Even though one does not have to agree fully with their classification, their overview communicates the notion that no single instrument will be the cure-all for ailing economies quite well. The area where venture capital is said to potentially have the greatest effect is the "development of inputs for using industries," such as software and instruments, while the "development of complex systems," for instance in the aerospace or semiconductor industry, is better left to R&D cooperatives that include large established firms that can better exploit economies of scale and scope.[25]

Lastly, Hall (2002) looks closely at financial market transaction costs and shows how these can lead to underinvestment in R&D even when one does not take the externalities sketched above into account. Among other things, he argues that an undersupply of R&D can result from asymmetric

[22]For more details, consult David et al. (2000: 526, table 5).

[23]Wallsten (2000: 83)

[24]In yet another twist, however, Audretsch et al. (2002: 145) conclude that "there is ample evidence that the DoD's [Department of Defense's] SBIR Program is stimulating R&D as well as efforts to commercialize that would not otherwise have taken place."

[25]See Martin and Scott (2000: 439, table 1).

information. When an inventor with an insufficient internal cash-flow turns to the capital markets to finance a long-term research project whose riskiness is not easily assessable for outsiders, then debt financing is often difficult to secure because lenders demand a high interest rate in return for the high risk they incur, up to the point where a credit cannot be secured at all and the project has to be abandoned.[26]

Based upon his review of the literature, Hall (2002: 45) concludes that "there is solid evidence that debt is a disfavored source of finance for R&D investment." Moreover, "the evidence from Germany and some other countries suggests that small firms are more likely to face [debt-financing] difficulty than large established firms."[27] Of special interest here is Hall's argument that venture capital might help overcome such problems by mitigating asymmetric information problems and that it can thus lead to more inventive activity by small and medium-sized businesses.

On a final, related note, Belke et al. (2005) find econometric evidence for the notion that a more vibrant venture capital sector positively influences the labor market even if one does not take R&D efforts into account directly. In their seminal paper on the macroeconomic link between venture capital disbursements and labor market performance, they find that venture capital investments tend to reduce the economy-wide unemployment rate notably. In order to give an idea of the magnitudes involved, Belke et al. (2005: 120) offer an example, stating that "[i]n Germany, a 100 percent increase in venture capital [invested] in 1997 [...] would have lowered the level of the unemployment rate by something more than 1 percentage point and thus would have created around 380,000 new jobs by 1999."[28]

[26]See Stiglitz and Weiss (1981) for a description of the underlying mechanisms and Martinelli (1997) for a more recent application.

[27]Hall (2002: 45). See Holmstrom (1989) for a theoretical elaboration.

[28]Note that the overall new private equity disbursement volume in Germany stood at approximately €1.21 billion in 1997, meaning that – according to this result – one additional job in 1999 could have been created via an investment of just €3168.64 in 1997.

2.4 A strong case for public intervention

A report by the U.S. Congress' Committee on Science and Technology concluded in 1985 that "[i]n general, the process of commercializing intellectual property is very complex, highly risky, takes a long time, costs much more than you think it will, and usually fails."[29] Given such formidable obstacles and the pervasive market failures in R&D discussed above, a strong case for an active public policy in the venture capital sector can be made.

Under the reasonable assumption that every government would like to induce higher rates of economic growth, and based on the insight from endogenous growth theory that the main driver of growth in advanced countries is its society's ability to generate and commercialize ideas, fostering an active venture capital market appears to be an especially apt instrument for increasing overall welfare. The existing studies conclude unanimously that venture capital-backed research is more effective than corporate R&D, so the potential effect of a public dollar spent on fostering venture capital activity outweighs the effects of a dollar spent on subsidizing corporate R&D.

An objection at this point might be that there is no reason to assume that venture capitalists will target the sectors of the economy that produce the highest social return to R&D. Indeed, the exact opposite will probably be the case: venture capitalists will target those industries where *private* returns to R&D are highest. Unless the government wants to engage in research itself, however, subsidizing venture capital-backed R&D will likely often represent the best alternative for fostering growth, and one that is more often than not superior to subsidizing corporate R&D.

The main question that thus remains is how exactly a more active venture capital market can be "created." Should public policy try to induce more demand for venture capital, or should supply be targeted? This question will guide us through the next chapters.

[29]Quoted in Bozeman (2000: 627).

Chapter 3

Venture capital in the U.S.

3.1 History of venture capital in the U.S.

The modern venture capital industry came into being in 1946, when MIT president Karl Compton, Harvard Business School professor Georges F. Doriot, and local business leaders from the Boston area founded American Research & Development (ARD).[1] ARD's goal was to help commercialize technology developed during the Second World War, and what made ARD "modern" was the fact that in addition to simply providing capital to start-ups, assisting its portfolio firms with management assistance was also part of the plan from the very beginning.

One remarkable fact is that ARD was set up in order to meet a perceived need for venture capital. Many ideas were waiting to be commercialized, and quite a few of them were the offspring of research efforts during the war, including, but not limited to, radar, microwave technology, and aeronautics. Yet, more than a few were also the offspring of what Field (2003) has recently called "the most technologically progressive decade" of the 20th century, the years from 1929 to 1941.

[1] For a compact overview of the history of the U.S. private equity market see Fenn et al. (1995: 7-16). Gaida (2002: 86-174) gives a detailed overview of the history of the private venture capital market in the U.S.

Often overlooked, the 1930s were a decade of intense private R&D efforts in the U.S., as Field (2003: 1406, emphasis in original) points out:

> "National Research Council data show that between 1919 and 1928 inclusive, companies founded an average of 66 R&D labs per year. Between 1929 and 1936 inclusive, a period that brackets the worst years of the Depression, 73 on average were founded per year. During the 1930's, industry R&D expenditures more than doubled in real terms, with acceleration in the last years of the decade [...]. Mowery reports that employment of research scientists and engineers grew 72.9 percent between 1929-1933 while employment total in other occupational categories collapsed. Between 1933 and 1940, R&D employment in U.S. manufacturing almost *tripled*, from 10,918 to 27,777. In the Second World War, in contrast, research and development employment growth slowed as employment in other categories skyrocketed. Federal spending for nondefense R&D also fell substantially during World War II."

The stage for venture capital was thus set in the U.S. in the mid-1940s. Yet, despite the favorable world ARD was born into, it had a turbulent life.[2] What made it successful in the end was by and large a single home run, a $70,000 investment in computer firm Digital Equipment Corporation (DEC) in 1957 that over time grew to a handsome $355 million.[3]

It took a while for the first limited partnerships, the venture capital fund structure of choice nowadays, to arrive on the scene. Only in 1958, Draper, Gaither & Anderson came into existence, and its novelty lay in the fact that the venture capitalists were the general partners of the fund, while outside investors became limited partners, in effect allowing the circumvention of the stringent Investment Company Act of 1940.[4] However, not much else went on in the 1950s and 1960s; the market remained in an embryonic phase

[2]Gaida (2002: 40-60) provides a detailed summary of ARD's history.

[3]See Gompers and Lerner (1998c: 152).

[4]See Bartlett (1995, 1999) and Callison (2000) for an introduction to the legal – mainly liability and tax – considerations that play a special role in the venture capital market.

until the late 1970s. Then, in 1979, the U.S. Department of Labor clarified how the "prudent man" provision in the 1974 Employee Retirement Income Security Act (ERISA) could be interpreted by pension funds, and this opened the floodgates for a massive new supply of money to the venture capital industry.[5] Ever since, pension funds have been the single most important group of limited partners in the U.S. venture capital market. However, the U.S. venture capital market only witnessed a real explosion of activity from the mid-1990s on, as discussed below.

This is not to say, however, that the venture capital industry was unimportant in the U.S. before the mid-1990s. A quick look at the companies which received venture capital-backing in those still relatively quiet days reveals how profound an impact it already had while it was still relatively small. In the high-tech realm, the list includes, among others, Microsoft, Intel, Cisco Systems, Sun Microsystems, America Online, Netscape, Amgen, Dell Computer, Genentech, Compaq Computers, and Yahoo! Inc. Some well-known companies in the service sector that received venture capital-backing at one point include Federal Express, Staples, and Starbucks. Taken together, the market capitalization of only the twenty most valuable venture capital-backed companies in the U.S. stood at $1.861 trillion on December 31, 2000. Put differently, it was one percent higher than Germany's 2000 GDP.[6]

[5]See Gompers and Lerner (1998c) for an econometric analysis of the impact of ERISA's clarification in 1979 and Hauser (2003) for an introduction to ERISA's legal intricacies as they relate to venture capital.

[6]Market capitalization data is taken from Gompers and Lerner (2001a: 71, table 4-4). The market value of all public, formerly venture capital-backed U.S. firms stood at $2.7 trillion year-end 2000 (Gompers and Lerner 2001a: 68, table 4-2), eclipsing the *total* public market capitalization in Germany by a factor of 2.

3.2 Venture capital in the U.S. in the 1990s and beyond

Before delving into the depths of the statistical tables provided by the NVCA and BVK, we first need to take a closer look at the categories of data reported in the NVCA Yearbook. The four main categories include early stage financing – i.e., seed and start-up financing –, expansion financing, later stage financing, and acquisition/buyout financing. While all four categories certainly fall under the heading private equity, only the former two comprise true venture capital. As we will see in chapter 4, the *BVK Statistiken* report the data for Germany for four largely similar categories: early stage, expansion, specialized later stage, and MBO/MBI/LBO. As far as they are comparable, again only the first two categories constitute true venture capital and will serve as the basis for comparison between the two countries that chapter 5 is concerned with.

In the following, data for "real venture capital," meaning only seed, start-up, and expansion financing, is presented. All information is taken from the 2004 NVCA Yearbook and is reported from 1991 on to allow for comparability with the German data, which is only available from then on; also note that the numbers reported in earlier NVCA Yearbooks need not always match those presented here. Some words on terminology: "new funds raised" refers to how much money investors, such as pension funds and banks, have pledged to venture capitalists in any given year. "Capital under management" designates the total volume of funds that venture capitalists have at their disposal.[7] "Disbursements" are all investments made in a given year, not adjusted for exits. It is thus equivalent in meaning to "new money invested." Finally, "total funds invested" designates how much money venture

[7] In the case of the NVCA, this figure is calculated as follows: "Our industry definition of capital under management is the cumulative total of committed capital less liquidated funds or those funds that have completed their life cycle." (NVCA 2001: 17) The BVK pursues a different approach, surveying firms every year on funds under management and then adding this information up to arrive at total funds under management.

capitalists have cumulatively invested in the firms currently in their portfolio, using the book value of these investments as the basis.[8]

Using the approach outlined above, a perusal of the 2004 NVCA Yearbook yields the information contained in figure 3.1 to 3.3, and the data appendix presents the underlying data in numerical form. Last but not least, table 3.1 shows the sectoral breakdown of U.S. venture capital sources for 1998-2003.

Further descriptive statistics on the current state of the U.S. venture capital industry have been compiled by the consulting firm Global Insight, Inc. (2004).[9] Among other things, the report states that currently or formerly venture capital-backed companies in the U.S. employed 10.1 million workers in 2003 and had sales totalling $1.8 trillion in the same year. Remarkably, even after the burst of the high-tech bubble, these firms reported a job growth of 6.5% from 2000-2003, while sales rose by 11.6% over the same period.

Table 3.1
Sources of U.S. venture capital funds, 1998-2003

	1998	1999	2000	2001	2002	2003
Pension funds	60.16%	43.50%	40.10%	41.70%	42.21%	43.07%
Financial and insurance	10.36%	15.50%	23.30%	24.50%	25.52%	24.73%
Corporations	11.87%	14.20%	3.70%	2.60%	2.32%	1.92%
Endowments and foundations	6.31%	17.21%	21.10%	21.80%	20.88%	20.53%
Individuals and families	11.31%	9.61%	11.80%	9.40%	9.06%	9.76%

Source: NVCA Yearbook (2004).

[8] Those interested in a more in-depth discussion of the U.S. venture capital industry in the 1990s than is provided here should refer to Lerner (2000), Gompers and Lerner (1999, 2001a), and Gaida (2002). Other sources of current information on the U.S. venture capital market include the NVCA Yearbooks (yearly), the Pricewaterhouse-Coopers/Thomson Venture Economics/National Venture Capital Association MoneyTree Survey (www.moneytree.com), the *Venture Capital Journal*, and two online databases provided by VentureEconomics and VentureOne. Availability of the latter sources outside the U.S. is very limited, however.

[9] A booklet containing the highlights of their report "Venture Impact 2004: Venture Capital Benefits to the U.S. Economy" are available for download from the NVCA website.

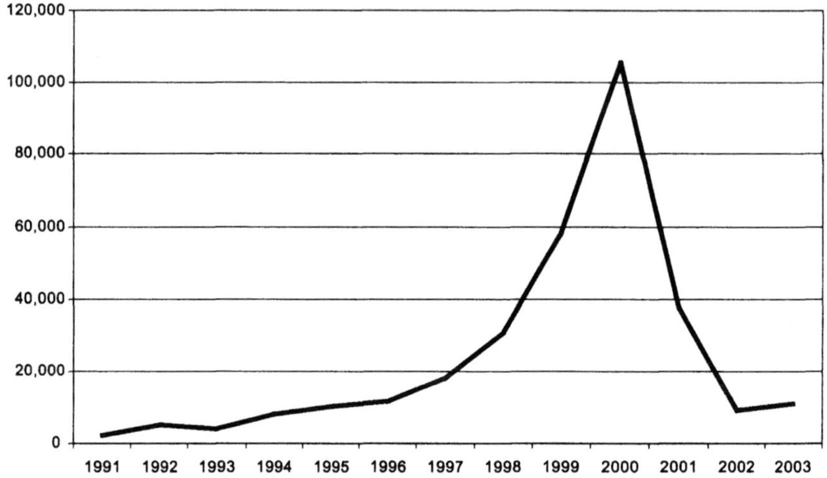

Figure 3.1
New U.S. venture capital funds raised (in million $), 1991-2003
Source: NVCA Yearbook (2004).

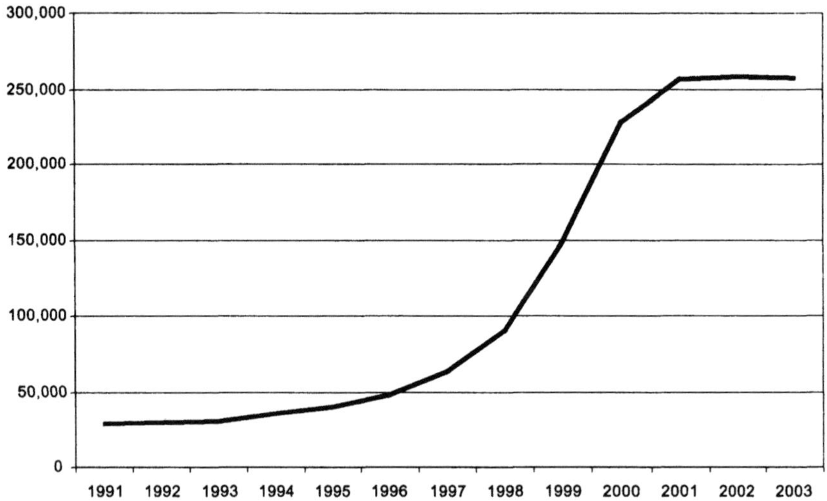

Figure 3.2
U.S. venture capital under management (in million $), 1991-2003
Source: NVCA Yearbook (2004).

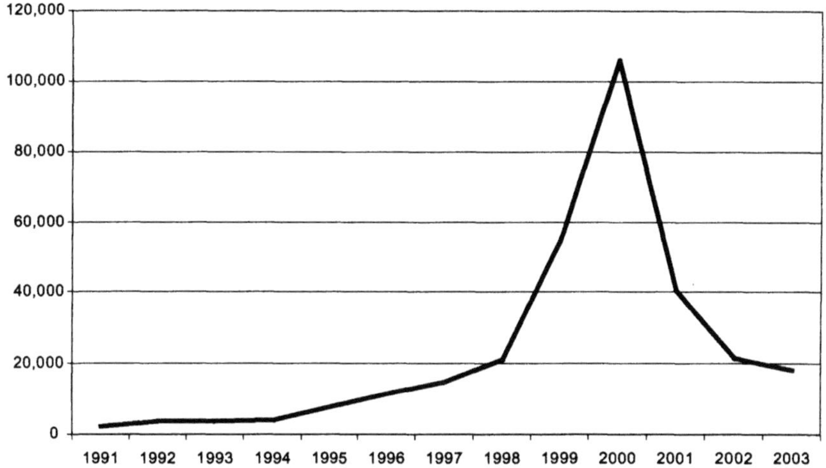

Figure 3.3
U.S. venture capital disbursements (in million $), 1991-2003
Source: NVCA Yearbook (2004).

3.3 U.S. government programs

The first explicitly venture capital-related government programs for fostering technology-oriented companies came into existence at an easily predictable time, namely in 1958, not long after the 1957 launch of the *Sputnik* satellite had created fears that the Soviet Union might be about to gain a relative edge over the U.S. in the technology sector. The program, called the Small Business Investment Company (SBIC) program,[10] was initiated as part of the Small Business Investment Act of 1958 and to this day operates under the auspices of the Small Business Administration (SBA).[11]

[10]See Gaida (2002: 61-95) and Noone and Rubel (1970) for a comprehensive overview of the early history of the SBIC program.
[11]It is important not to mix up the SBICs with the unrelated SBIR (Small Business Innovation Research) program, despite the easily confused acronyms.

To cut a long story short, the SBICs did not meet with the success that Congress had hoped for when it initiated the program. Fenn et al. (1995: 8) observe:

> "A third defect of the SBIC program, and the most damaging, was that the program did not attract investment managers of the highest caliber. In June 1966, an outgoing deputy administrator of the SBA startled the venture capital community and the Congress by declaring that the SBA was likely to lose $18 million because of the 'wrong people who operate SBICs.'"

Gordon (1998: 50) points to a problem of similar magnitude that resulted when SBICs made use of debenture financing, meaning that they refinanced themselves under preferred terms via the SBA:

> "While the debenture program made the SBIC program popular after its formation in 1958, the drawbacks of the debenture program helped lead to the decline of the SBIC program by the early 1990s. The main disadvantage of the debenture program was the fundamental mismatch of using debt financing to fund equity investments. On one side, the SBA demanded semiannual interest payments from the SBICs. On the other side, the SBA encouraged SBICs to make equity investments in small businesses. Yet by their nature, these equity investments produced unpredictable cash flows – or no cash flows whatsoever – until a final liquidity providing event such as an IPO or acquisition of the small business. Thus, a debenture-financed SBIC that pursued a strict equity investment focus faced the risk of bankruptcy in the short-term, even though in the long term its investments might prove highly lucrative."

Overall, the actual design of the SBIC program turned out to be a less effective mechanism for providing capital to small technology-oriented companies than had been planned. Despite the fact that major revisions of the program were implemented in 1992, once more Gordon (1998: 54) on balance observes that "[t]he SBIC program is no longer needed in today's venture capital market." As we will see in chapter 4, close parallels with German efforts to foster venture capital activity abound, and what is true for the SBIC program is quite likely also a valid description of most government-backed schemes in Germany:

> "The costs of the SBIC program probably far exceed the benefits. First, administering the SBIC program requires an enormous bureaucracy and significant resources. [...] Second, there is a major governmental cost from SBICs that are unable to repay their financial obligations to the SBA. [...] A *Wall Street Journal* study revealed potential 1990s SBIC losses exceeding $800 million. [...] In 1996, the government earned a total of $695,000 in SBIC profit sharing. That same year, the SBA's liquidation losses were $1.3 million."[12]

The second major program targeted at small businesses, and thus indirectly beneficial to the U.S. venture capital market, is the Small Business Innovation Research (SBIR) program, which has disbursed more than $7 billion to small businesses between 1993 and 1997.[13]

Lerner (1999) provides an extensive discussion of this program, and I will thus limit the discussion here to a quick review of his main conclusion. Altogether, he provides an upbeat assessment, noting that "[t]he SBIR awardees enjoyed substantially greater employment and sales growth" than firms in a non SBIR-sponsored control group.[14] He also finds that receiving an SBIR grant increases the likelihood of obtaining venture capital-backing later on, a fact which he ascribes to the potential certification role of the SBIR awards.

[12] Gordon (1998: 53)

[13] Lerner (1999: 285). Other well-known – albeit somewhat smaller – programs, such as Sematech and the Department of Defense's Advanced Technology Program, will not be discussed here because not enough relevant literature on them is available so far. For more information, see Lerner's (1999: 287-289, table 1) comprehensive overview of the multitude of programs created by U.S. government agencies.

[14] Quoted from Lerner (1999: 315).

Nonetheless, as already noted above under 2.3, Wallsten's (2000) rigorous analysis of the SBIR program casts serious doubt on its effectiveness. Specifically, he asks "whether the program encourages managers to fund research that benefits society but is privately unprofitable. I find evidence that the program does not encourage such behavior. Instead, it appears to reward the funding of commercially viable projects."[15] Put differently, the SBIR program seems to have no positive net effects on the innovative activity of small businesses and can thus not cause any positive spill-overs to the venture capital industry.

It should come as no surprise that numerous other programs exist or existed in the U.S. that target the small-business sector.[16] After all, there is an old saying that if U.S. politicians can agree on one thing, then it is that motherhood, home-ownership, and small business activity should all be encouraged. Yet, a detailed discussion of these activities is of course beyond the scope of this book. The interested reader is therefore referred to Lerner (1999: 287-289, table 1), where a three-page overview of the major public initiatives related to venture capital that were in place between 1958 and 1997 is provided.

Altogether, it seems fair to say that one view pervades the literature with regard to the U.S. government's desirable role in the venture capital sector. Florida (1994: 27) neatly summarizes it as follows: "[T]he venture-capital industry does not need the government's help, and the government certainly does not have what it takes to be a venture capitalist."

[15] Wallsten (2000: 83)

[16] One interesting description of a fringe program – aimed at creating state-certified venture capital companies backed by insurance companies, or CAPCOs for short – can be found in Barkley et al. (2001).

Chapter 4

Venture capital in Germany

The financing of entrepreneurial activity in Germany has a long tradition, and at least reaches back to medieval times, when vast trading empires, such as those associated with the Hanse and Fugger, blossomed in regions that are now part of Germany. The advent of modern venture capital firms is a much more recent phenomenon in Germany, though. Only by the mid-1960s the first Kapitalbeteiligungsgesellschaften (KBGs - equity stock companies), which can loosely be regarded as the German counterpart to the U.S.' SBICs, were founded. Finally, nearly another two decades later, in 1983, the first independent, U.S.-style venture capital firms came into being in Germany.

The relative novelty of venture capital in Germany is reflected in the literature. Few studies of the early days of venture capital in Germany exist, and those that do often sketch pictures which are markedly different from each other.[1] Nevertheless, in this chapter an attempt is made to sum up what is known about venture capital in Germany at the aggregate level, and the data presented here is compared to that for the U.S. in chapter 5. In addition, part 4.4 of this chapter is devoted to a broad-strokes description of the major policy initiatives that were implemented with the aim of strengthening the German venture capital market.

[1]The best available studies on the early years of venture capital in Germany include Gaida (2002), Harrison (1990), and especially Leopold and Frommann (1998).

4.1 The emergence of the modern venture capital industry in Germany

The earliest signs of modern venture capital activity in Germany became visible in the mid-1960s. The first private KBGs were founded from 1965 on, often with backing from commercial banks, and include, to name just a few of the more prominent ones, the "Deutsche Beteiligungsgesellschaft mbH" (1965), the "Allgemeine Kapitalunion GmbH & Co KG" (1966), the "KBG Kapitalbeteiligungsgesellschaft mbH" (1968), the "GeBeKa, Gesellschaft für Beteiligungen und Kapitalverwaltung mbH & Co" (1969), and the "Beteiligungsgesellschaft für die deutsche Wirtschaft mbH" (1969).[2] In addition, between 1966 and 1976, another 11 funds were set up that predominantly received their capital from publicly-held banks, namely the 11 *Landesbanken* that operated in Germany at the time.[3] Of the 33 venture capital companies that were founded between 1965 and 1972, 20 remain in business today, of which only six are still considered relevant players.[4]

Even though many of the KBGs had relatively few problems raising funds given their strong ties to large banks, they made few successful investments. They mostly restricted themselves to holding equity stakes in already established, albeit innovative firms (as *stille Gesellschafter*) and generally tried to avoid risky investments. Not surprisingly, their reputation was quickly tarnished, as many thought that the KBGs "expected highest returns without risk."[5] By the mid-1970s, however, the KBGs had changed their strategy somewhat and now increasingly assumed a more active role in their portfolio firms and even started to think about stock market IPOs as exit venues.[6]

---

[2]For a comlete list, see Leopold and Frommann (1998: 43-45), who also report that the first KBG in Germany, the "BONA Kapitalbeteiligungs-GmbH & Co. KG," was founded in June 1965 by a group of private investors lead by a lawyer. It went bankrupt in 1970.

[3]The first fund backed by a *Sparkasse* was the "S-Siegerlandfonds," which began its work on October 31, 1983; see Brunswig (1984).

[4]Leopold and Frommann (1998: 47)

[5]Frommann (1992: 104, own translation)

[6]IPOs never played an important role at the time, though; see Frommann (1992: 104).

The most prominent government-backed initiative of the time, the "ERP-Beteiligungsprogramm," which was initiated on September 4, 1970, is important for two reasons. On the one hand, it was the first program that had as its aim offering below-market rate refinancing options to KBGs and also assumed a disproportionate amount of the risk associated with a given investment. More concretely, 75 percent of the investment made by a KBG could be refinanced via the *Kreditanstalt für Wiederaufbau* (KfW), at a subsidized annual interest rate of 5%, and up to 70 percent of the investments could be secured by governmental guarantees.[7] At the same time, the program was by-and-large unsuccessful.[8] The ERP-backing came with a series of stringent requirements, among them the requirement that investments should be "hands-off," that rendered reliance on this source of capital unattractive for profit-oriented KBGs.

Combined, these two aspects are especially important as public policies designed to foster more venture capital activity in Germany still largely rely on those concepts that already failed in the 1970s. Not surprisingly, the aim of one of the latest schemes, a €500 million ERP/EIF fund set up by the German government in collaboration with the European Investment Fund in early 2004, aims at "crowding in" private investment, too. Whether it will be more successful than its 1970 predecessor remains to be seen.

After the first rough years, which saw several bankruptcies and acquisitions, the private equity scene had managed to establish a secure foothold in the German economy by the mid-1970s. In 1975, €215 million had been invested in 367 SMEs.[9] The next landmark event, the creation of the "Deutsche Wagnisfinanzierungs-Gesellschaft mbH" (WFG) falls into the same period. Prompted by government demands for easier access to high-risk financing options, in 1975 28 German banks teamed up and contributed equity capital to the WFG, while the German government initially agreed to absorb 75

[7] See Leopold and Frommann (1998: 48-53) for details.
[8] Frommann 1992: 104
[9] Frommann 1992: 105

percent of all potential future losses.[10] The WFG was initially capitalized at €5.11 million, which was subsequently raised to €25.56 million.[11]

Despite initially high hopes,[12] numerous problems, not least a too cautious and narrow investment approach, plagued the WFG from its very beginning, and it quickly ran into problems. After a streak of losses amounting to (cumulatively) €19.84 million by the end of the fiscal year 1980/81 – compared to investments totalling just €16.57 million –, major restructuring was deemed necessary, not least because the taxpayer now actually had to shoulder 75 percent of the losses, or €14.83 million.[13]

From 1981 on, the WFG was overhauled repeatedly, culminating in a "new" WFG that was to operate entirely with private backing, i.e., without any government guarantees and risk-sharing schemes. It started its work in 1984 and had only five shareholders.[14] As Harrison (1990: 132) notes: "The differences between the 'new' and the 'old' WFG included a larger fund pool and a visible change in investment policies: later stage investments took priority over early stages and start-ups; no longer were specific branches preferred over all others; non-tech investments were more frequent; and foreign investment and co-venturing were introduced." These reforms, while pointing in the right direction, once more proved less successful than expected, though, so that Deutsche Bank finally bought out the other four remaining partners in 1988 and made the WFG part of its subsidiary *Deutsche Beteiligungsgesellschaft mbH*, one of Germany's oldest KBGs.[15]

The year 1983 finally marked the arrival of independent, privately held venture capital firms in Germany that tried to emulate the business practices and investment strategies of their counterparts in the U.S. Among the firms that entered the scene were GENES/IVCP, Techno Venture Management

[10] Harrison (1990: 131). This arrangement expired on September 30, 1984.

[11] Frommann (1992: 105). Gaida (2002: 235-245) presents an extensive case study of the WFG that goes far beyond the overview given here. Moreover, refer to Becker and Hellmann (2005) for an in-depth discussion of the myriad problems the WFG faced.

[12] These are very clearly reflected in Gerke (1975) and Stoehr (1976), for instance.

[13] Büschgen (1985a: 224)

[14] Industriemagazin (1985: 146)

[15] Harrison (1990: 132-33)

Table 4.1
Early development of the German private equity market

Year	# of venture capitalists reporting data	# of investments total	# of investments private	# of investments ERP-backed	total funds invested in million € total	total funds invested in million € private	total funds invested in million € ERP-backed	disburse-ments in million €
1975	24	340	194	146	190	168	22	na
1979	na	684	208	476	286	198	87	na
1980	na	910	220	690	317	215	102	na
1981	na	978	233	745	346	243	102	na
1982	na	1,055	255	800	385	259	126	na
1983	na	1,069	246	823	401	266	135	na
1984	31	1,127	302	825	438	314	124	na
1985	44	1,277	380	897	516	382	134	na
1986	52	1,429	467	962	695	545	150	210
1987	60	1,583	578	1,005	814	652	162	215
1988	na	1,683	597	1,086	1,125	866	143	298
1989	na	1,752	735	1,017	1,318	1,130	188	377
1990	na	2,111	890	1,221	1,739	1,538	201	ca. 511
1991	80	2,410	1,136	1,274	2,113	1,853	260	551
1992	84	2,665	1,283	1,382	2,623	2,325	299	628
1993	84	2,758	1,266	1,492	2,748	2,411	337	517
1994	85	2,942	1,306	1,636	3,158	2,731	427	740
1995	87	3,093	1,313	1,780	3,204	2,717	487	583

Source: Adapted from Leopold and Frommann (1998: 80, table 2).

(TVM), and the KBG Berlin, followed by several other companies in 1984-1987.[16] These new firms decided to focus first and foremost on backing young high-tech firms with considerable growth potential, a clear break with the low-risk approach of the past. Yet, over time it became clear that in order to cover management fees and the day-to-day expenses of the new venture capital funds, investments in later-stage ventures were desirable, too, as these paid dividends much more quickly and thus helped sustain the new firms through the first, often dire years.[17]

[16]Frommann (1992: 105). The TVM was backed, among others, by Siemens AG and T. A. Associates, an experienced venture capital firm based in Boston (Wirtschaftswoche 1983). On the history of GENES – and its formal parent IVCP, whose main office was located in Luxemburg for tax reasons – see Nathusius (1989).

[17]Frommann (1992:106)

Table 4.2
Fundraising and investment activity in the German private equity market in the early and mid-1980s

Year	Yearly data		Cumulative development		
	Investments (million €)	Projects	Funds raised (million €)	Investments (million €)	percent invested
1980	1,53	5	30.68	11.76	38.3
1981	2,56	6	30.68	14.32	46.7
1982	1,48	13	31.70	15.80	49.8
1983	21.88	29	110.95	37.68	34.0
1984	73.52	62	284.53	111.21	39.1
1985	71.99	92	452.54	183.20	40.5
1986	77.36	109	583.38	260.55	44.7
1987	103.54	119	756.71	364.09	48.1

Source: Own presentation based on Harrison (1990: 154, table 4-6; 155, table 4-7).

In order to get some sense for when a viable venture capital industry took hold in Germany, pre-BVK estimates must be used. Fortunately, Leopold and Frommann (1998) provide a rather comprehensive overview of the situation in the 1980s (table 4.1). Another data set that is much less comprehensive in many respects is provided by Harrison (1990). It is nonetheless included here because it also reports fundraising activity and allows the calculation of the percentage of funds invested relative to the funds available to venture capitalists, which strikingly never exceeded 50 percent in the eight years for which data was collected (table 4.2).

The fund overhang observed by Harrison is echoed in other sources, too. A 1985 article in the Industriemagazin (1985) states that of the then available funds of €383 million only about 20 percent had actually been invested. Büschgen (1985b: 288), who estimates the supply of venture capital to be around €358 million in 1985, even claims that at most 10 percent of these funds appeared to have been invested at the time, indicating an even more pronounced fund overhang. While Schmidt (1988) reports higher investment volumes, namely €141 million in 1988, spread over 169 portfolio firms, compared to less than €511 million available funds, supply still clearly outpaces demand in this case, too.

Given these views, it is not surprising that the chairman of the BVK, Holger Frommann, already pointed out more than a decade ago that lack of supply never seems to have held back the development of the German venture capital market.[18] Both the fact that most KBGs could draw upon funds when needed by turning to the banks that owned them and the figures on capital inflows vs. disbursements make clear that, once the first venture capital firms had been established in Germany, the bottleneck has not been a lack of available funds, but rather an apparent lack of qualified demand.

The last source that sheds some light on venture capital activity in Germany in the 1980s is the European Venture Capital Association (EVCA) Yearbook *Venture Capital in Europe 1987*. Overall, it takes a very optimistic view, introducing its chapter on Germany with the statement: "Venture capital in Germany came into its own in 1986."[19] The second paragraph, which is worth quoting in its entirety, is equally upbeat:

> "German venture capital activities are characterised by the changing attitude of entrepreneurs. The year 1986 demonstrated that significant changes are beginning to take place; the owners and managers of small and medium-size companies are becoming more aware of growth as a central strategy for their enterprises. Gradual, long-term development, very low turnover rates of employees and the central role of a founding personality are slowly giving way to a market-driven orientation that requires a high degree of professional management experience. Only when this orientation becomes the accepted mode of strategic thinking can venture capital financed enterprises begin to appeal to the highly skilled

[18] Frommann (1993: 14, own translation) states: "Contrary to the manifold claims of a lack of supply of risk-seeking capital in Germany, it can be said that capital earmarked for investments in private equity always has been and still is available in sufficient quantities." Gaida (2002: 225, own translation) argues very similarly: "The supply of capital – unlike in the U.S. – never seems to have been an obstacle for equity participation schemes [in Germany]. Banks provided (their) KBGs with sufficient capital, which often was – and even still today is – not invested completely."

[19] EVCA (1987: 39)

groups of middle managers in the larger corporations, who have so far elected to stay on the sidelines instead of joining the management teams of start-ups."[20]

The key numbers reported by the EVCA for 1986 (1985) are €231.38 million "new funds raised," €678.79 (451.14) million "capital under management," €111.10 (208.49) million "disbursements," and €412.82 (346.34) million "total funds invested."[21] Altogether, the EVCA (1987: 42) reports: "Excluding the activities of the traditional investment companies reveals that venture capital funds alone accounted for DM 785 million [€401.36 million] of total funds available for investment, for DM 120 million [€61.36 million] of total investments made and for 264 out of 1,171 investee companies."[22]

[20] EVCA (1987: 39)

[21] All data are taken from EVCA (1987). The exchange rates used are ECU 1 = €1.14089 for 1985 and ECU 1 = €1.06144 for 1986.

[22] The "traditional investment companies" referred to here include all KBGs.

4.2 Venture capital in Germany in the 1990s and beyond

The early 1990s mark an important event, if not for the venture capital market in Germany itself, then at least for the literature on it, as the BVK began publishing its yearly statistics in 1991.[23] These so-called "BVK Statistiken" constitute the closest approximation to "official" data that is available.[24] As the following discussion reveals, however, the state even of the more recent data prevents much in the way of clear-cut conclusions about long-term patterns in the German venture capital market unless great care is taken.

As will soon become clear, several data issues raise formidable barriers to sensible cross-country comparisons between the U.S. and German venture capital markets, yet few if any studies acknowledge these problems explicitly. While the venture capital market sprouted up later in Germany than in the U.S., it did appear quite a bit earlier than 1991, yet, as we have seen, the information so far available on earlier years leaves much to be desired, and valid comparisons with U.S. data pre-1991 are thus next to impossible.

Even if we temporarily content ourselves with the truncated series of official statistics, two other serious problems loom. The first arises from the fact, already noted, that the term "venture capital" is used differently on the two sides of the Atlantic: in the U.S., only seed, start-up, and expansion financing are subsumed under the venture capital heading, whereas in Europe venture capital is normally understood to include later-stage financing, such as buyouts and turnaround financing, as well. Controlling for this distinct usage is one of the aims of the following analysis. The second problem is even harder to overcome. Careful examination of the BVK statistics demonstrates that the figures presented there are unfortunately at times inconsistent both within years and over time.

---

[23] For an overview of the at times turbulent first years of the BVK itself, see the account by Leopold and Frommann (1998: 72-75).

[24] I will refer to the data reported in them as the "official data" in the following.

Below, the main results of an extensive analysis of the German data are reported. A compact summary of the numbers underlying the graphs can be found in the data appendix, and I accordingly refrain from reporting these in the form of tables in the body of the text. Unless otherwise noted, data for 1991 and 2001 and later refer to the data reported for BVK members only, while 1992 to 2000 figures are for the *Gesamtmarkt*, which includes all BVK members plus all other firms that have voluntarily reported their data to the BVK.[25] Whenever the term "real venture capital" is employed, it refers to the sum of seed, start-up, and expansion financing only and explicitly excludes later-stage activity, such as buyouts.

The data presented in the figures 4.1 to 4.4 includes all private equity. By contrast, the figures 4.5 and 4.6 report information for "real venture capital" only, meaning just seed, start-up, and expansion financing. Unfortunately, a breakdown along these lines over a longer period of time is only possible for disbursement volumes and cumulative funds invested, as the BVK only started to report the necessary fine-grained data on fundraising activity in 1999. Moreover, it stopped reporting cumulative data in 2000.

Last but not least, the tables 4.4 and 4.5 provide a broad-strokes overview of the German regions and industries that have attracted the most attention from private equity firms in the past. This information is included here mainly for completeness' sake. Useful further discussions of many topics that are not explicitly covered here, for example of the developments in the geographic area that until 1990 made up the German Democratic Republic (the so-called *Neuen Bundesländer*), can be found in the monograph by Leopold and Frommann (1998: 75-206).[26]

[25]Since 2001, only data for BVK members is reported in the yearly *BVK Statistik*, as this information is said to be sufficiently representative of the market as a whole (see the announcement in the BVK Statistik 2001 (published in 2002), page 2).

[26]Frommann and Dahmann (2003) also provide additional information on the relevance of the current German private equity market for specific market segments, such as the biotechnology and telecommunications sectors, and for the German economy as a whole.

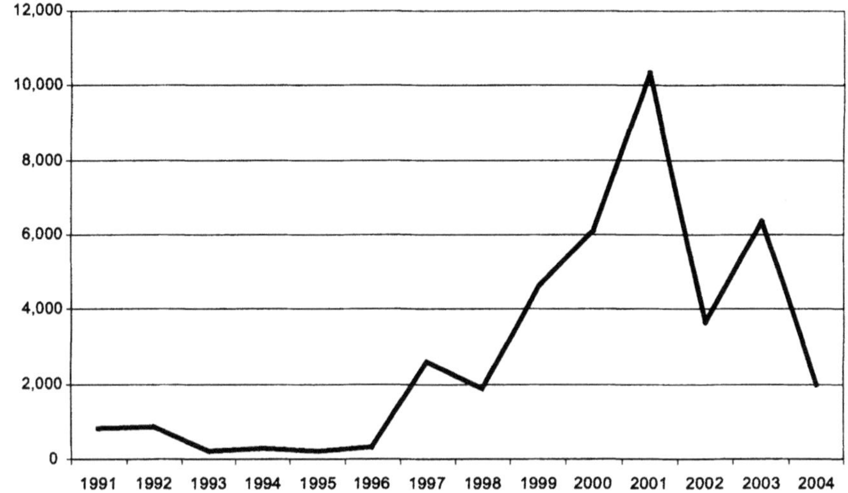

Figure 4.1
New German private equity funds raised (in million €), 1991-2004
Source: BVK Statistik, various years.

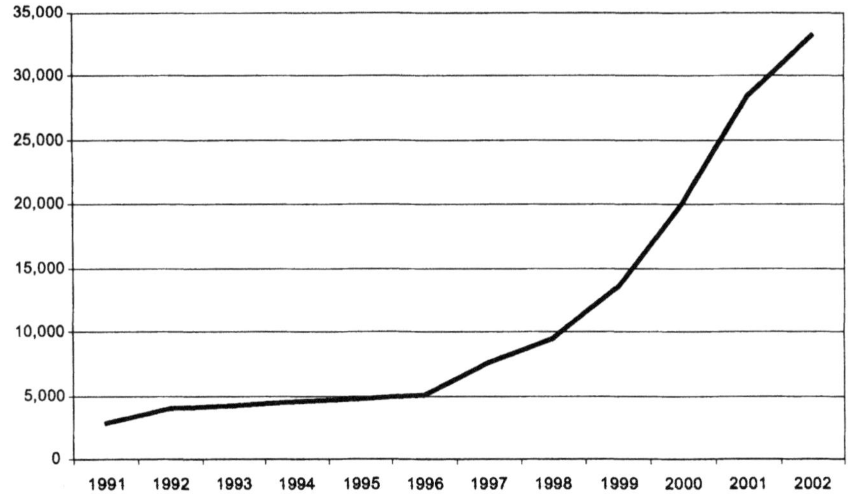

Figure 4.2
Private equity under management in Germany (in million €), 1991-2002
Source: BVK Statistik, various years. (Data is only available until 2002.)

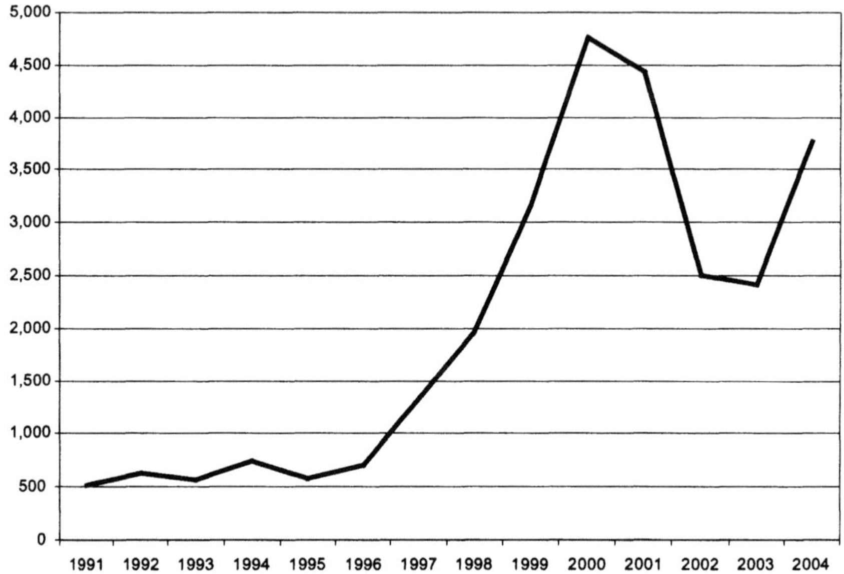

Figure 4.3
German private equity disbursements (in million €), 1991-2004
Source: BVK Statistik, various years.

4.3 Data problems

Having presented a lot of data on the German private equity market, the manifold problems with these figures should not go unmentioned. Among the data problems already alluded to earlier, the influence membership changes in the BVK have on the reported figures is most unsettling. Membership changes can largely be regarded as exogenous shocks and thus distort the data considerably. Some venture capital firms only join the BVK after a few years, others join as soon as they are founded, and yet others drop out because they went bankrupt. As the following table 4.7 makes clear, the changing basis for measurement renders valid inference using time-series approaches virtually impossible unless great care is taken.

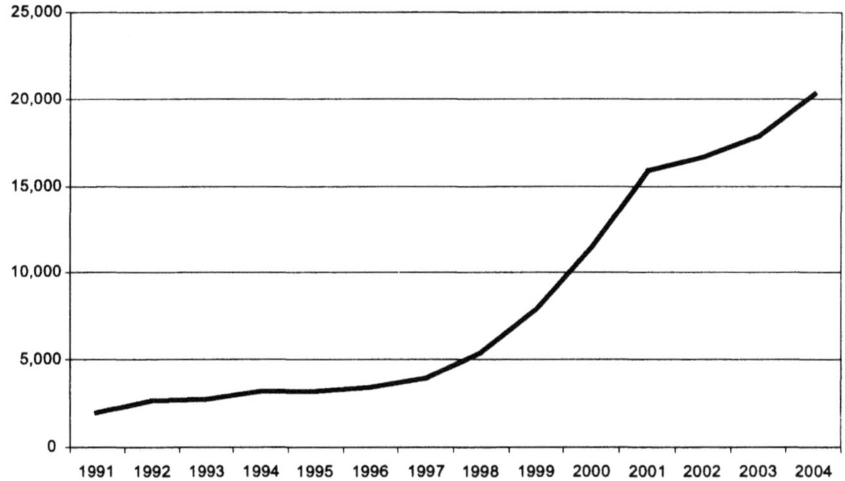

Figure 4.4
Total funds invested in Germany (in million €), 1991-2004
Source: BVK Statistik, various years.

Table 4.3
Sources of German private equity funds, 1999-2004

	1999	2000	2001	2002	2003	2004
Financial companies	31.96%	28.90%	17.70%	21.60%	11.10%	19.50%
Insurance companies	9.14%	16.34%	16.90%	13.80%	10.10%	30.50%
Pension funds	22.87%	5.74%	28.00%	39.10%	24.10%	0.00%
Industrial firms	8.55%	8.65%	9.10%	3.50%	1.10%	2.30%
Private investors	9.22%	10.60%	11.60%	2.60%	5.10%	4.00%
Public sector	11.55%	16.39%	5.70%	10.60%	4.10%	16.40%
Academic institutions	0.00%	0.00%	0.30%	0.00%	0.00%	0.00%
Re-investments	0.23%	0.24%	0.00%	1.30%	1.50%	8.10%
Funds of funds	4.32%	7.19%	10.60%	5.80%	1.20%	5.5%
Capital market	na	na	na	na	0.10%	3.60%
Other	2.16%	5.95%	0.10%	1.60%	41.60%	10.00%

Source: BVK Statistik, various years. (Note: Percentages for 1999 and 2000 are for the Gesamtmarkt, 2001-2004 data are for BVK members only.)

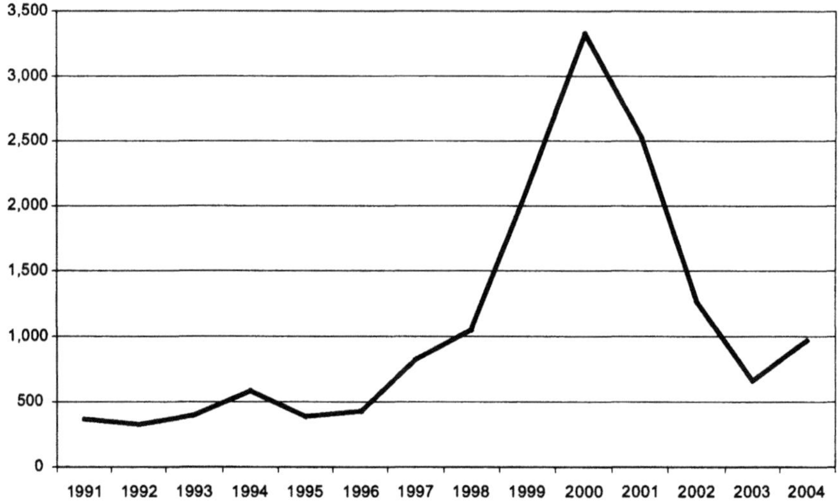

Figure 4.5
German real venture capital disbursements (in million €), 1991-2004
Source: BVK Statistik, various years; own computation.

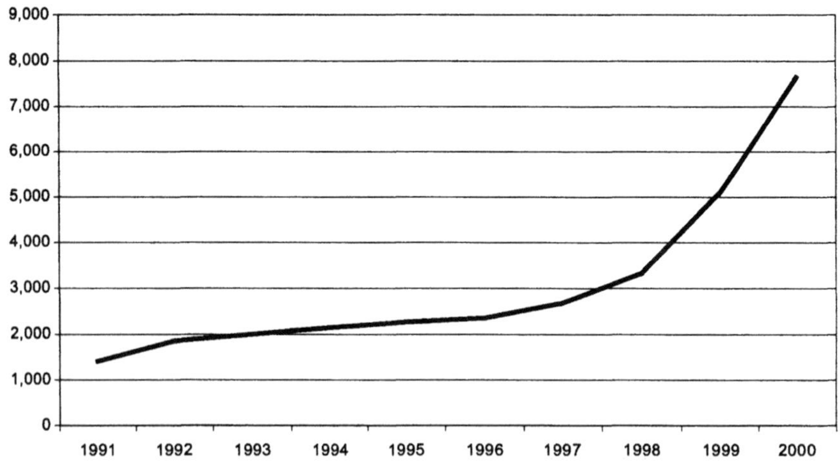

Figure 4.6
Cumulative German real venture capital (in million €), 1991-2000
Source: BVK Statistik, various years; own computation. (No data is available post-2000.)

Table 4.4
German private equity disbursements by geographical region, 1998-2004

	1998	1999	2000	2001	2002	2003	2004
Baden-Württemberg	14.13%	14.43%	13.07%	12.20%	19.10%	9.00%	16.40%
Bayern	24.60%	20.25%	19.93%	21.60%	17.10%	21.80%	27.80%
Berlin	4.54%	10.88%	11.14%	9.40%	5.30%	2.50%	3.30%
Brandenburg	2.79%	1.75%	3.14%	1.30%	1.00%	0.40%	0.10%
Bremen	1.42%	0.22%	0.58%	0.50%	0.40%	0.10%	0.10%
Hamburg	4.01%	5.24%	5.28%	5.00%	4.10%	18.20%	0.50%
Hessen	7.52%	9.01%	8.64%	15.40%	6.60%	3.90%	5.40%
Mecklenburg-Vorpommern	0.74%	1.14%	0.73%	0.40%	0.80%	0.40%	0.30%
Niedersachsen	3.16%	6.16%	4.29%	3.70%	24.70%	1.60%	13.60%
Nordrhein-Westfalen	25.94%	18.58%	19.99%	19.20%	10.60%	36.50%	27.60%
Rheinland-Pfalz	1.95%	2.39%	1.93%	4.40%	1.40%	1.00%	1.00%
Saarland	0.36%	0.59%	1.73%	0.40%	1.60%	0.90%	0.20%
Sachsen	4.54%	3.55%	4.32%	2.40%	2.10%	0.90%	1.20%
Sachsen-Anhalt	0.84%	1.18%	1.50%	1.00%	1.60%	1.50%	1.00%
Schleswig-Holstein	2.15%	1.80%	1.79%	1.90%	1.20%	0.70%	0.50%
Thüringen	1.31%	2.83%	1.94%	1.20%	2.20%	0.60%	0.90%

Source: BVK Statistik, various years; all percentages refer to BVK members only.

To see the problem more clearly, consider the year 2001. The BVK Statistik 2002 reports that the total portfolio value that German private equity firms held on December 31, 2000 was €10,701.3 million, while the value of the portfolio of all BVK members stood at €13,264 million just one day later (January 01, 2001). This jump of €2,562.7 million in total portfolio size was simply due to the fact that new members joined the BVK, but does not reflect any real activity in the market. By contrast, the market witnessed some real investment activity over the course of 2001, amounting to €2,580 million. If we now compute the ratio of the shock due to membership changes relative to real investment activity, this yields a value of 99.33 percent.

In other words, relative to real activity, nearly as much of the "change" witnessed from year-end 2000 to year-end 2001 is due to a more or less random event. Equally troubling is the fact that the numbers in the BVK statistics sometimes do not add up in a way that standard arithmetic would suggest; simply unexplainable gaps in the data are not uncommon.[27]

[27] To give just one example: in 1995, new funds raised by BVK members are reported

Table 4.5
Sectoral breakdown of German private equity disbursements, 1998-2004

	1998	1999	2000	2001	2002	2003	2004
Agriculture / Forestry	0.00%	0.00%	0.16%	0.10%	0.10%	0.00%	0.00%
Chemical	4.06%	1.77%	1.34%	15.30%	17.00%	6.70%	1.80%
Iron / Steel / Light metals	2.76%	1.38%	0.67%	1.00%	2.50%	2.40%	2.00%
Machinery	10.85%	9.84%	6.37%	11.30%	17.20%	7.50%	9.30%
Energy	0.20%	0.34%	0.28%	1.20%	0.60%	0.60%	1.30%
Electronics	4.12%	2.79%	2.01%	2.40%	7.20%	1.60%	2.90%
Industrial Automation	1.42%	2.41%	2.44%	1.20%	1.70%	3.80%	2.60%
Computer - Hardware	3.90%	4.27%	2.46%	0.80%	1.50%	0.50%	0.20%
Computer - Software	10.73%	14.94%	20.61%	14.20%	8.60%	4.30%	2.60%
Computer - Semiconductors	na	0.26%	2.95%	1.40%	1.20%	1.00%	0.30%
Communications Technology	4.65%	11.63%	11.65%	8.20%	6.50%	11.50%	3.00%
Biotechnology	8.00%	7.63%	11.09%	11.20%	8.60%	4.40%	4.00%
Medicine - Technical	4.32%	2.38%	2.03%	2.70%	2.20%	1.30%	3.60%
Medicine - Health care	na	1.12%	1.16%	1.10%	1.30%	1.00%	10.40%
Medicine - Pharmaceutical	na	0.76%	1.81%	1.60%	2.40%	1.40%	5.80%
Environmental Technology	2.80%	0.87%	0.78%	0.60%	0.60%	3.50%	1.20%
Consumer Goods	8.61%	7.40%	9.70%	11.00%	6.00%	3.70%	10.90%
Construction	2.94%	1.02%	1.25%	1.70%	2.30%	0.40%	0.60%
Retail / Wholesale	3.50%	4.86%	3.55%	3.30%	1.40%	4.20%	8.20%
Transportation	4.24%	0.52%	0.26%	0.60%	0.20%	5.80%	0.30%
Financial Services	0.58%	3.53%	4.93%	3.20%	0.60%	0.10%	0.30%
Hotels / Restaurants	5.60%	3.02%	0.12%	0.20%	0.20%	0.10%	0.10%
Other Services	6.11%	3.45%	7.12%	2.60%	3.10%	30.30%	17.90%
Other	9.44%	7.30%	5.07%	3.10%	7.10%	4.00%	10.60%

Source: BVK Statistik, various years; all percentages refer to BVK members only.

All these findings raise serious doubts about the validity of the few existing statistical and econometric studies on the German venture capital market. Unless both the data that the BVK provides is interpreted correctly and checked for accuracy and unless exogenous shocks are properly controlled for, we have to be very skeptical of any results that such studies produce. Unfortunately, even some of the most diligent researchers take German data at

to be DM 1,069.17 million, while the figure for the (more comprehensive) *Gesamtmarkt* is just DM 393.28 million. In 1994 the same problem exists, albeit on a smaller scale; the BVK members are said to have raised DM 586.91 million, while the *Gesamtmarkt* reportedly raised only DM 570.73 million. As the BVK members are a subset of the *Gesamtmarkt*, some of these numbers must be wrong. However, as there is no way to obtain more accurate data, all figures are reported here exactly as they appear in the yearly *BVK Statistiken*.

face value, it seems. The best book on venture capital, for example, "The Venture Capital Cycle" by Gompers and Lerner (1999), reports in table 1.5 on page 16 that the volume of early stage investments in Germany was $116 million in 1995 in 1997 US dollars. Gompers and Lerner cite a 1998 working paper by Jeng and Wells as their data source, which in turn appears to use EVCA data as its basis. The EVCA, finally, simply reported the faulty data the BVK furnished on the *Gesamtmarkt.* However, if we go back to the original BVK data, we see that the new early stage investment was DM 719.69 million (€389.42 million) in 1995. Given that the exchange rate of the USD was $1 = DM 1,7348 in 1997, Gompers and Lerner (1999) thus underestimate the German investment activity by approximately 350 percent.[28]

Table 4.6
Distortion of the German fundraising data due to BVK membership changes

Year	1991	1992	1993	1994	1995	1996	1997
Change†	−3.78%	23.12%	−34.52%	18.64%	11.13%	4.24%	−4.76%
Year	1998	1999	2000	2001	2002	2003	2004
Change†	6.55%	11.10%	12.55%	99.33%	36.59%	−23.49%	0.00%

†membership effect as percentage of total "real" portfolio change during year
Source: Own computation based on the BVK Statistiken, various years.

[28] "Early stage investment" is here taken to refer to the sum of seed, start-up, and expansion financing. Exchange rate data is taken from Deutsche Bundesbank, "Devisenkurse an der Frankfurter Börse," Zeitreihe WJ 5009, available online at http://www.bundesbank.de/stat/zeitreihen/html/wj5009.htm

4.4 German government programs

Despite many good intentions, public policy schemes to foster a more vibrant venture capital market in Germany have proven frustratingly unsuccessful so far. Citing an OECD study, Gompers and Lerner (2001a: 16) remark dryly: "In Germany [...], more than 600 government programs encouraged venture activity between 1965 and 1995, with few appreciable benefits."[29] Indeed, if there is one common theme that unites the myriad initiatives in Germany, it is their apparent lack of success.

The later disappointments notwithstanding, as early as 1983 a conference jointly organized by the German Ministry for Research and Technology and Berlin's Senator for Trade and Transport was held to examine the German venture capital market, its likely future development, and the potential obstacles it would have to overcome on its way to maturity. The subsequently published 284-page conference volume makes clear that the German government took an active interest in this capital market segment very early on and at least pledged to design effective public policies to foster it.[30]

As it is of course not feasible to review in detail the several hundred programs that the German government instituted over the years, I will focus on the broad ideas behind them whenever possible.[31] However, a short review of the central initiatives is in order here. Before providing this review, though, a mere enumeration of the more recent major public initiatives that have immediate relevance for the venture capital market in Germany will give a good impression of why only a broad-strokes approach is possible:[32]

[29]The report they cite is OECD. 1995. *Government Programmes for Venture Capital*. Paris: OECD. I was neither able to obtain a copy in Germany nor in the U.S., but believe the quote to be accurate.

[30]Workshop Venture Capital für Junge Technologieunternehmen (1983). This interest was also reflected in the business press; see Wirtschaftswoche (1983).

[31]See Güllmann (2000: 263-333) for a detailed overview of the major initiatives.

[32]I have refrained from translating the program titles here for ease of readability.

- Gesetz zur Förderung von Wagniskapital,
- Drittes Finanzmarktförderungsgesetz,
- Kapitalaufnahmeerleichterungsgesetz,
- Gesetz zur Fortentwicklung der Unternehmenssteuerreform 2001,
- BMF-Schreiben zur Fondsbesteuerung, den Carried Interest-Altfällen und der Umsatzsteuer auf Management Fees (Dezember 2003),
- EU-Wertpapierdienstleistungsrichtlinie,
- Gesetz zur Kontrolle und Transparenz im Unternehmensbereich,
- various programs administered by the Deutsche Ausgleichsbank (DtA) (and its subsidiary Technologie-Beteiligungsgesellschaft (tbg)) and the Kreditanstalt für Wiederaufbau (KfW), including:
  - Förderprogramm "Beteiligungskapital für kleine Technologieunternehmen,"
  - DtA-Technologie-Beteiligungsprogramm,
  - FUTOUR (Förderung und Unterstützung von technologieorientierten Unternehmensgründungen in den neuen Bundesländern und Ost-Berlin),
  - ERP-Beteiligungsprogramm,
  - KfW-Beteiligungsfonds Ost,
  - KfW-Risikokapitalprogramm.

In terms of the broad overview alluded to above, Gaida (2002) traces the roots of government schemes targeted at German private equity firms back to the late 1960s. As already discussed under 4.1, at around the same time the so-called "ERP-Beteiligungsprogramm" was initiated. Its aim was to provide capital to small and medium-sized enterprises indirectly: KBGs, already discussed above, were allowed to borrow at subsidized rates from the ERP program in order to be able to supply more funds to small and medium-sized enterprises – an approach that persists until the present day, even though the current programs bear different labels.[33] However, the program quickly proved unpopular and inefficient, as the KBGs preferred to invest in stable and moderately risky firms, while the ERP funds were mainly earmarked for the financing of innovative projects.[34] Moreover, what has been said in the context of U.S. SBICs quite likely applied to the German KBGs, too:

> "[T]here is an adverse selection problem among SBIC managers. Those venture capitalists with the best track records and reputations do not need to resort to SBA funding. Venture capitalists who do seek SBIC licenses probably do so because they lack private market alternatives. This pattern suggests that SBIC funds, on average, may be managed by the least qualified venture capitalists in the industry."[35]

A second explicit attempt to promote private equity activity in Germany was made in the mid-1970s. In 1975, the WFG, which was again already introduced above, was set up to meet a (governmentally) perceived demand for venture capital. It is important to keep in mind that the WFG was not a public entity, even though public pressure was conducive to its creation. Yet,

---

[33]See Bruhns (1992) for a comprehensive discussion of the main characteristics of the pre-1990 public policies aimed at KBGs (and here especially the so-called *mittelständischen* KBGs). Overall, his predominantly descriptive assessment of the effects of these policies appears too optimistic, though, and is not shared widely.

[34]Gaida (2002: 230). As Frommann (1993: 13) correctly points out, the KBGs that still operate today have typically become much more risk-seeking and are hardly distinguishable from other venture capital firms.

[35]Gordon (1998: 54)

the German Ministry for Research and Technology agreed to bear 75 percent of all potential future losses that the WFG might incur and in return the WFG was supposed to invest only in high-risk ventures that could not find any other financing sources.[36] Another explicit aim was to help commercialize results from publicly sponsored R&D projects. In the end, however, the WFG faltered due to a whole array of reasons, not the least being mismanagement.

Gilson (2002: 42) neatly sums up the problems that plagued the WFG: "In short, WFG was a government program that created a financial intermediary that had no incentives, did not monitor, involved the government, through board representation, in project selection and, not surprisingly, produced dismal results."

In stark contrast, Gaida (2002: 275-294) portrays the more recent public initiatives in the private equity sector as much more successful. The three initiatives that he discusses are the "Förderung technologieorientierter Unternehmensgründungen (TOU)," which was in place from 1983 to 1988, "Beteiligungskapital für junge Technologieunternehmen (BJTU)," which ran from 1989 to 1994, and the program "Beteiligungskapital für kleine Technologieunternehmen (BTU)," which was initiated in 1995. Indeed, these programs, which offer re-financing opportunities and investment guarantees and make use of co-investment schemes, were certainly more successful than the ERP program and the WFG, but it is still unclear by how much.

Unfortunately, Gaida fails to present data that conclusively strengthens his claim of increased efficiency, nor do any other econometric studies of these programs seem to exist.[37] In fact, with respect to the BJTU program, an OECD (1997: 24) report remarks: "It is subject to debate whether this low failure rate [17 percent] may reflect an overly cautious approach; the government may be too concerned with only picking winners, with the result that many inventions do not make it to market." Indeed, the 17 percent

[36] Frommann 1992: 105

[37] See also Güllmann (2000), who attempts a tentative qualitative evaluation of these programs. One pervasive concern that both he and Gaida (2002) for some reason do not address sufficiently are selection effects.

failure rate reported by the OECD compares very favorably to the current "market rate," which stood at 41 percent in 2004.[38]

One feature that all the newer initiatives discussed above share is that – in time-honored fashion – the supply of venture capital is clearly targeted. As a look at the actual data presented in this book strongly suggests, however, insufficient demand rather than supply seems to be the main force holding back the German venture capital market, and chapter 7 thus returns to this issue at some length. In addition, under the current supply-side policy one might also observe an adverse-selection effect, meaning that only the least qualified private equity firms actually rely on the government's help, while the better ones have no problems to meet their financing needs via private markets. In turn, the not-so-good firms could then outbid their better peers, which could ultimately lead to *lowered* social welfare, as the management assistance that the publicly-backed firms provide is inferior to that of their privately-backed peers, giving rise to less successful portfolio companies.

[38] 252 out of 615 exits were listed in the category "total write-offs." See the BVK Statistik 2004, table A16 ("Exitkanäle 2004").

Chapter 5

Venture capital in the U.S. and Germany in comparison

This chapter sets out to provide a valid quantitative comparison of the venture capital activity in the U.S. and Germany. So far, to my knowledge no such comparison exists. The goal of this comparison is to make clear where the German venture capital market stands relative to its counterpart in the U.S. Against this backdrop, it becomes possible to evaluate public policy for venture capital, which is the ultimate goal of the lengthy data analysis presented so far.

As will soon become clear, the German venture capital market is not trailing the American one by as much as many assume, and lack of demand in both countries is as visible in the 1990s as it was in the 1980s data presented for Germany in the last chapter.

5.1 Market size relative to GDP

To assess the relative size of the venture capital markets in the U.S. and Germany, the data for "real venture capital" in both countries is here standardized by current GDP. Doing this avoids measurement bias with respect to both inflation and exchange rate fluctuations. Regrettably, in the case of commitments the BVK did not report the necessary data prior to 1999, so only a seriously truncated time-series for 1999 to 2004 can be computed. The data appendix provides an overview of all data used below, including references to the sources of GDP and public equity market capitalization (PEMC) information.

Without doubt, the U.S. venture capital market is considerably larger than its German counterpart, even after normalizing by GDP. Interestingly, the gap between the two markets has widened since the mid-1990s until 2000. However, following the old adage that what goes up must come down, the gap has narrowed again from 2001 onwards.

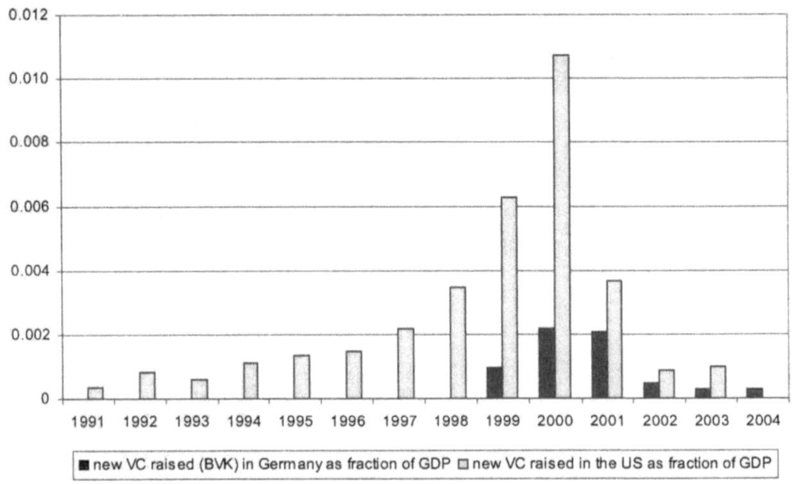

Figure 5.1
Venture capital commitments relative to current GDP, 1991-2004
Source: BVK Statistik, various years, NVCA Yearbook (2004); own computation.

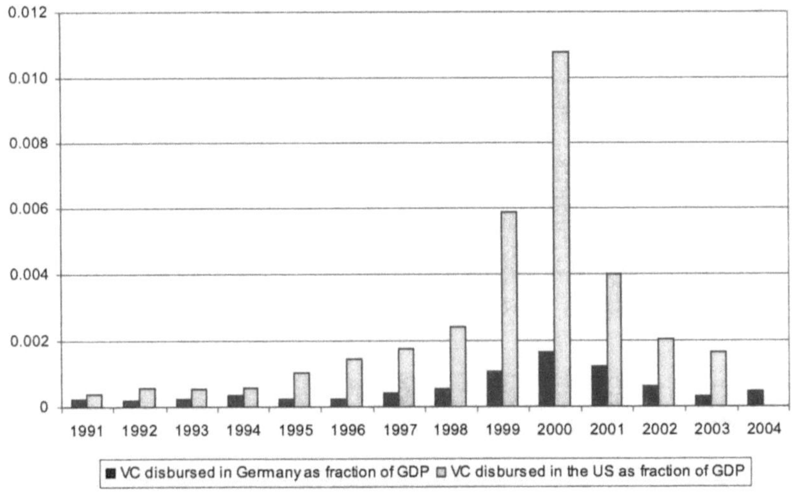

Figure 5.2
Venture capital disbursements relative to current GDP, 1991-2004
Source: BVK Statistik, various years, NVCA Yearbook (2004); own computation.

5.2 Market size relative to the stock market

If we use another measure, public equity market capitalization instead of GDP, to normalize the venture capital data, Germany even comes out ahead in 2001 and 2002 when it comes to fundraising. This result certainly is surprising to many who lament the allegedly dismal state of the German venture capital scene – and especially to those who see lack of supply as its root cause –, even though they might rightly point out that relative to GDP a lot of catching-up still lies ahead. Even though the weighting of venture capital data by PEMC data for the U.S. and Germany is somewhat unusual, it can *prima facie* be justified by noting that differences in investors' risk aversion between the two countries could account for a smaller venture capital market in Germany. However, this lack-of-supply story does not hold up well against the evidence presented at the end of this chapter.

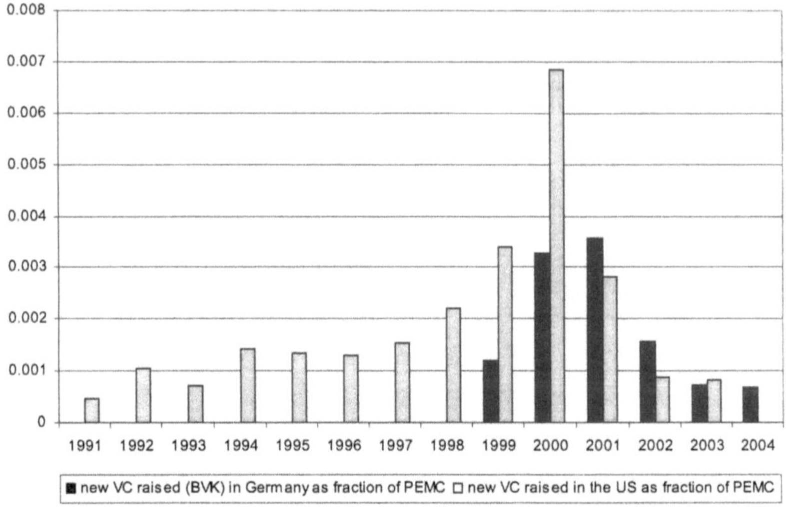

Figure 5.3
Venture capital commitments relative to PEMC, 1991-2004
Source: BVK Statistik, various years, NVCA Yearbook (2004); own computation.

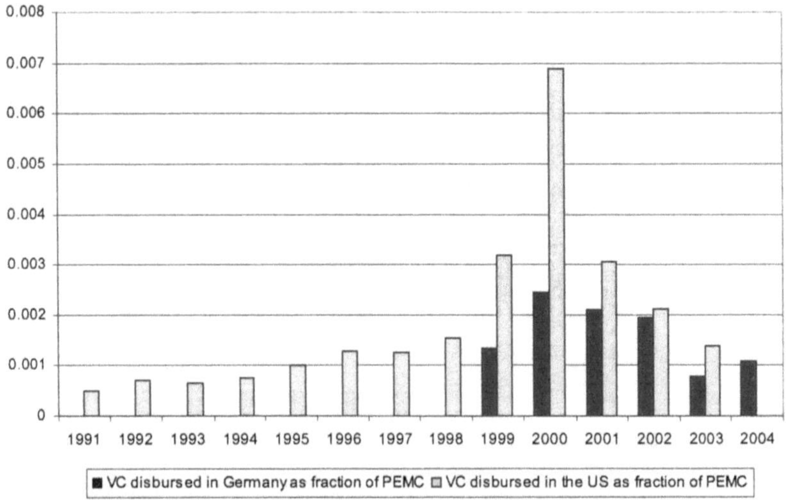

Figure 5.4
Venture capital disbursements relative to PEMC, 1991-2004
Source: BVK Statistik, various years, NVCA Yearbook (2004); own computation.

5.3 Disbursements relative to commitments

Once all the above computations are carried out, we have a valid comparison of the size of commitments and disbursements for the German and U.S. venture capital markets. Yet, some last figures have to be calculated, namely those for supply of capital relative to demand. As data on how much of the money committed in a given year was earmarked for venture capital funds is not available for Germany for most of the 1990s, we are once again faced with a severely truncated time-series.[1]

Upon closer scrutiny, an interesting pattern emerges from figure 5.5. As we saw in the discussion of the 1980s data on Germany in chapter 4, generally more capital is pledged to venture capitalists than is normally invested. This pattern can clearly be discerned for the U.S. during the 1990s, as well.[2] Since 2000, actual investment has outpaced the inflows of funds into the industry, a sign that venture capitalists are eager to finally put at least some of their reserves to work. For Germany, a similar picture emerges. In 2000 and 2001, inflows of capital exceeded new investments in portfolio companies, hinting once more at lack of demand. Since 2002, however, German venture capitalists have also begun to reduce their overhang of funds and currently invest more than they raise. Simultaneously, at the moment one looks in vain for complaints about lack of available funds, which strongly suggests that supply of capital to the industry is not a pressing problem, either. Rather, the slower pace of investing of the already available funds when compared to the U.S. once more points towards a lack of qualified demand for venture capital in Germany.

Disturbingly, as Cornelius (2005) and Züchner (2003) have rightly pointed out, the overhang of funds might even be damaging to Germany's innovative capacity. Venture capital firms seem to react to a overhang of funds by investing larger sums per deal and the median valuation of deals thus increases notably. By contrast, the fraction of the earliest stages – seed and start-up

[1] Once more, see the data appendix for the underlying data.

[2] 1991 is the one exception to this rule.

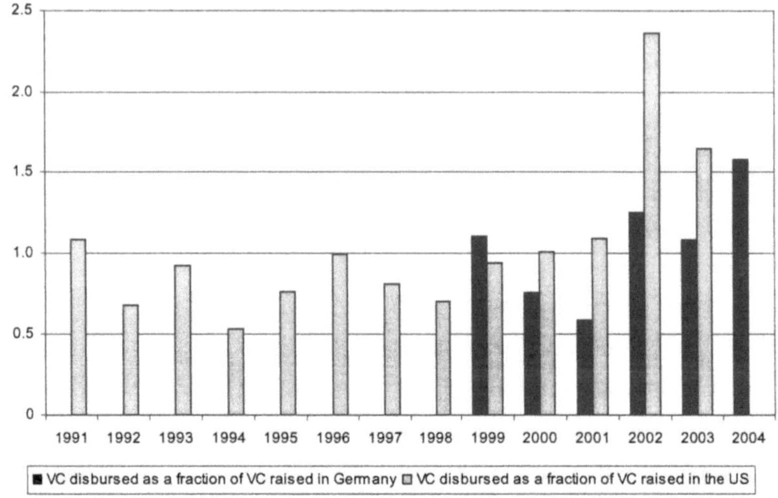

Figure 5.5
Venture capital disbursements relative to commitments, 1991-2004
Source: BVK Statistik, various years, NVCA Yearbook (2004); own computation.

investments –, falls. In Germany, for instance, in 1997 10.1% (27.0%) of all venture capital deals were struck for seed (start-up) investments, while by 2001 this fraction had fallen to 3.9% (22.1%). Finally, in 2004 only 2.7% of all deals fell into the seed-financing category, while the start-up fraction had rebounded to 34.7%.[3] When one looks at the absolute numbers, the inverse relation between fund overhang and seed financing is even more obvious: In 1997, 164 firms received seed-financing, in 2001 just 103, and by 2004 this number had dropped to a dismal 26. In other words, "too much" available capital apparently can make venture capital firms weary of (too many) small deals. The prevalent German public policy of trying to expand the pool of available capital even further is thus potentially self-defeating and might at worst even have harmful consequences.[4]

[3]For the U.S., see the NVCA Yearbook 2004, page 32.

[4]Absent more concrete firm-level evidence of a change in behavior that is induced by a fund overhang, one should be careful about drawing such a conclusion, however.

Chapter 6

IPOs and venture capital

6.1 Existing views on stock market exits and venture capital

The literature on venture capital has identified three main reasons for why IPOs could play an important role in the venture capital cycle. These are:

1. IPOs on average generate significantly higher ROIs than other divestment venues,

2. entrepreneurs value the possibility to regain control over their firm via an IPO, and

3. IPOs signal that a given venture capital manager is successful and thus help raise follow-on funds.

All three arguments are rigorously and at length scrutinized below. Eventually, it will become clear that neither the first nor the second argument are theoretically convincing, while the third one at least matches the empirical record well.

IPOs cause higher returns and thus more inflows

The view that IPOs generate the highest returns on a given venture capital investment is widespread. The NVCA has issued several studies which show that returns are by far highest on average when venture capital-backed firms go public. The two other divestment mechanisms, trade sales and buybacks, are on average far less profitable, even though occasionally trade sales can cause some headlines, too.[1]

Sahlman (1990: 478, table 1 continued) gives an overview of the relative frequency of IPOs vs. trade sales in the years 1980 to 1988. He finds that in all but two years, 1981 and 1983, trade sales were more frequent than IPOs. He does not provide us with a breakdown of the relative volume of the deals, though, and I suspect that in terms of total amounts raised IPOs were the most important means of divestment in all years, with the possible exception being the year 1988.

At the risk of being not very representative, a snapshot look at some figures from the NVCA Yearbook 1989 (NVCA 1990: 42) reveals: "The average valuation for the 25 private companies with disclosed acquisition valuations last year [1989] was $71.3 million, a 37% increase from the $52.1 million average of the 37 private companies with disclosed valuations in 1988. The median valuation last year was $40 million, up from $16.7 million." Compare this to an average IPO offering valuation of $100 million for 1989 and $91.8 million for 1988 (NVCA 1990: 44, Figure 4.0). Likewise, the report continues: "While this [acquisitions] is a consistent exit vehicle for venture capitalists, studies done by Venture Economics have shown that returns from IPOs generally exceed those achieved through acquisition by a wide margin."[2]

[1]For instance, Hellmann (2000: 2) cites the case of Cerent, which was acquired in a private deal by Cisco Systems for an impressive $6.9 billion. Of course, a write-off is another exit mechanism (percentage-wise even a rather important one – at least 20 percent of all investments are on average written off, in bad times as much as 40 percent), but in terms of value this venue of course equals zero, so I will not discuss this possibility any further.

[2]NVCA (1990: 43)

Indeed, the literature often cites a 1988 study by Venture Economics titled "Exiting Venture Capital Investments," which according to Gompers and Lerner (1998b: 160-161) reports the following: "A 1988 Venture Economics study found that a $1.00 investment in a firm that goes public provides an average cash return of $1.95 in excess of the initial investment with an average holding period of 4.2 years. The next best alternative, an investment in an acquired firm, yields a cash return of only 40 cents over a 3.7 year mean holding period."[3] Strikingly, this 1988 study is still widely quoted, which might well mean that there is no newer data set out there.

One rather extensive data set on IPOs vs. trade sales is reported in Gompers and Lerner (1999: 215, table 11.1). What becomes clear from their table is that the average size of IPOs in the biotech sector is more than five times (roughly 5.2 times) that of acquisitions. This calculation is based on 136 IPOs with a total volume of $4.044 billion and 614 acquisitions with a total volume of $3.521 billion, both for the period from 1978 to September 1992. Finally, the following passage from Gompers and Lerner (1999: 205) is largely representative of the prevailing views in the literature on IPOs and venture capital:

> "Perhaps the clearest illustration of the relation between the private and public markets was seen during the 1980s and early 1990s. In the early 1980s, many European nations developed secondary markets. These sought to combine a hospitable environment for small firms (e.g., they allowed firms to be listed even if they did not have an extended record of profitability) with tight regulatory safeguards. These enabled the pioneering European private equity funds to exit their investments. A wave of fundraising by these and other private equity organizations followed in the mid-1980s. After the 1987 market crash, initial public offering activity in Europe and the United States dried up. But while the U.S. market recovered in the early 1990s, the

[3] I was neither able to obtain a copy of this study in Germany nor in the U.S.

> European market remained depressed. Consequently, European private equity investors were unable to exit investments by taking them public. They were required either to continue to hold the firms or to sell them to larger corporations, often at relatively unattractive valuations. While U.S. private equity investors – pointing to their successful exits – were able to raise substantial amounts of new capital, European private equity fundraising during this period remained depressed."

Note that this passage always refers to private equity, not just venture capital. The former includes the whole buyout market, and not surprisingly a stock market exit is often vital for that segment. Moreover, the authors talk about correlation, but fail to demonstrate causality.

Interesting as all the observations so far may be, they beg two main questions. First, are potential future IPOs really a factor that venture capitalists take into account when financing a company that is still in an embryonic phase, i.e., at the seed or start-up stage?[4] In accordance with the larger literature on IPOs, there is by now a consensus that venture capital-backed companies have to play by the rules of the stock market, too, so IPOs during times when the "window" is shut are few and far in between (1988 is a good example, as are 2002 and 2003). Can venture capitalists anticipate correctly what the stock market will look like in four or more years and invest accordingly? These questions have been tackled only half-heartedly so far, but at least Jeng and Wells (2000) and once again Gompers and Lerner (1998c) provide some thought-provoking answers, which I will return to after my discussion of the second question in the following paragraph.

Second, and I think most importantly, could the different average valuations and returns not simply reflect some characteristics of the venture capital-backed companies, i.e., the best ones are taken public, while the

[4]A much more pressing concern for many investors in seed- and other very early-stage firms might be whether they will be able to sell their stakes in their portfolio firms to other private equity outlets that focus on later-stage financing. See Murray (1994) and Michael D. Smith (2001).

merely well-to-do ones are sold to other companies? It might be hard to believe, but this question has not yet been seriously discussed in the literature. If IPOs are really a cure-all, then it is hard to understand why, according to the statistics in the 2000 NVCA Yearbook (p. 12), acquisitions were still more important in terms of overall proceeds than IPOs even at the height of the last IPO craze: "Exits during 1999 through both acquisitions ($35.6 billion) of venture-backed companies and initial public offering ($20.9 billion in proceeds) were at all-time record levels."

On a related note, many studies on the (alleged) advantages of IPOs seem to assume that the value of a venture capital-backed firm is determined by something other than its expected future cash-flow. Several papers find that venture capital-backed firms are underpriced during IPOs – Gompers (1996: 141) reports typical underpricing of around 10 percent –, so they are sold at a discount. Thus, assuming that an acquirer is willing to pay a fair value (the NPV), acquisitions should be more profitable, not less, all else equal.[5]

Despite the many theoretical holes in the IPO/venture capital argument, most researchers still readily accept the idea that IPOs are the crowning glory of the venture capital cycle. A quote from Shepherd and Zacharakis (2001: 60) is representative: "Sahlman (1990) documents that almost all of the returns on venture capital funds are earned on companies that go public [NB: Sahlman actually only quotes the Venture Economics study referred to above]. Bygrave and Timmons (1991, p. 159) note that 'hot IPO markets are by far the most important cause of peaks in venture capital returns.'"

Even though the latter observation is certainly correct, what really counts at the time of allocating funds between a set of possible investments is venture capital's performance vis-a-vis other securities, however, and one is left to wonder what good it is if the five-year rolling average returns on venture

[5]Loosely related is one aspect mentioned by Gompers and Lerner (1998a: 3). They find that venture capital-backed "[i]ssues underwritten by investment banks that are also venture investors are sold at a greater discount ('underpriced')." This potentially has some implications for Germany, as banks are some of the most active contributors to venture capital funds, which could in turn mean that IPOs on average have to be more underpriced in Germany, depressing returns and leading to a smaller venture capital market.

capital investments rise from 26.8 to 48 percent from one year to the next (as happened in 1998/99), when during the same period returns on less risky and much more liquid investment alternatives, such as the NASDAQ, shoot up by nearly the same amounts (see table 6.1). How exactly a "hot IPO market" will lead to a major reallocation of funds is not clear, then.[6]

Returning to the first question, in an empirical study that uses 1986-1995 panel data for venture capital markets in 21 countries, Jeng and Wells (2000) find an unambiguous, strong correlation between IPOs and venture capital activity for later-stage investments. They conclude: "Our results indicate that IPOs are the most important determinant of venture capital investing."[7] Further, when discussing their between regression result, they state that "[t]he coefficient on IPOs is positive and statistically significant for virtually all specifications. This lends support to the hypothesis [...] that high levels of IPOs in a country will lead to more venture capital."[8]

However, their results for early-stage investments, which they define as only including funds designated for seed and startup financing, are not as clear-cut. Again looking at their between regression results, they find:

> "It is surprising that the coefficient on IPOs in the early stage investment specification [...] is not significantly different from zero. This implies that countries with higher levels of IPOs do not have significantly higher levels of early stage investments as well. This is particularly puzzling in light of our results later on [...], which show that early stage investments are sensitive to IPOs over time."[9]

[6]See also Cochrane's (2005) careful discussion of the mean return, standard deviation, alpha, and beta of venture capital investments, which he finds to be comparable to those of the smallest NASDAQ stocks.

[7]Jeng and Wells (2000: 242)

[8]Jeng and Wells (2000: 266)

[9]Jeng and Wells (2000: 275)

Table 6.1
Five-year rolling averages for returns on investment in the U.S., 1990-2003

Year	venture capital	S&P 500	NASDAQ
1990	6.3%	9.4%	2.8%
1991	8.3%	11.5%	10.9%
1992	8.4%	12.0%	15.4%
1993	11.2%	10.9%	15.3%
1994	12.7%	5.4%	10.6%
1995	19.5%	13.3%	23.0%
1996	21.8%	12.2%	17.1%
1997	25.2%	17.4%	18.3%
1998	26.8%	21.4%	23.1%
1999	48.0%	26.2%	40.2%
2000	48.6%	16.5%	18.6%
2001	37.6%	9.2%	8.6%
2002	26.4%	−1.9%	−3.2%
2003	22.8%	−2.0%	−1.8%

Source: NVCA Yearbook (2004).

In contrast, when discussing their results for the within regressions, they report, "IPOs have a positive effect on the level of early stage investments from year to year. Thus, even though the average level of IPOs does not affect the amount of early stage investments [...], early stage investments are still affected by yearly fluctuations in the amount of IPOs."[10]

One should be careful when interpreting the results by Jeng and Wells (2000), though. The main caveat that applies here is that they might simply be measuring the importance of exit mechanisms overall, which would of course be reflected in their regression results. Strikingly, they leave out the second important such mechanism, namely trade sales, which potentially distorts their results significantly. As they themselves highlight:

[10] Jeng and Wells (2000: 276)

> "Since IPOs are significant in the fixed effects, within regression specification of Table 13, it is likely that we have not identified all the variables which affect early stage venture capital in the between regression. Another signal that we do not have all relevant variables is that the R-squareds for early stage investments, with a range of 0.15 to 0.68 (Table 10), are much lower than the R^2s for venture capital investment, which range from 0.49 to 0.71. One variable that might account for some of the unexplained variation is the amount of trade sales that take place. Trade sales are another exit mechanism, in addition to IPOs. We do not, however, at present have a measure for the prevalence of trade sales."[11]

Put differently, the main concern here is that IPOs might simply serve as a proxy for the importance of exits overall, whose significance should not surprise anyone.

In stark contrast to Jeng and Wells (2000), Gompers and Lerner (1998c: 167) assert in their comprehensive study of the U.S. venture capital industry:

> "Once other factors are included, the value of firms taken public by venture organizations in the previous year does not appear to have a dramatic effect on contributions. Although we cannot rule out a role for IPOs creating liquidity in the venture sector and potentially affecting contributions, we cannot find an effect in the multivariate regressions."

The dependent variable in their regressions is the natural log of commitments to new venture capital funds from 1969 through 1994, which they examine both for the U.S. overall and later on on a state by state and even fund-level basis, while "[t]he independent variables include the natural logarithm of the market value of firms brought public by venture organizations in the previous year (in millions of 1994 dollars), the real return on Treasury bills in the previous year, the real value-weighted stock market return in the

[11] Jeng and Wells (2000: 275)

prior year as reported by the Center for Research in Security Prices (CRSP), the previous year's real GDP growth, a dummy variable that equals one for years after 1978 when ERISA's prudent man rule was clarified, and the top marginal capital gains tax rate."[12] Once again, they do not include trade sales in their regression analysis.

To sum this section up, it should have become clear by now that no consensus on the importance of IPOs for the supply of venture capital exists. The two large-scale studies that exist, the ones by Jeng and Wells (2000) and Gompers and Lerner (1998c), reach strikingly different results. Maybe a lot of this is attributable to the different data sets they employ (24 countries vs. only one, 1986-1995 vs. 1969-1994), but in any case this is an area that certainly deserves further scrutiny, and the aim of the next section of this book is thus to shed some more light on the determinants of fundraising using the most recent data available. Also, the theoretical case for a strong link between IPO activity and venture capital fundraising, which too many uncritically accept, is not as strong as it could (and should) be.[13]

A final related train of thought is that venture capitalists could simply take companies public in another country. The Israeli venture capital industry pursued such an approach, and despite the languishing public equity markets in Israel, the venture capital industry there is among the most vibrant in the world. Much the same is true for Singapore, too. In this case, IPOs would still matter, but having a stock-market segment for young companies at home would make much less of a difference than many claim.[14]

---

[12]Gompers and Lerner (1998b: 164). One paper that actually does acknowledge the existence of both IPOs and trade sales as viable exit mechanisms and that models the choice between both theoretically is Hellmann (2000). He shows that sometimes acquisitions are the best choice, but does not provide any empirical data.

[13]Fiedler and Hellmann (2001) strongly argue against the view that stock markets play a central role in the venture capital fundraising process, too.

[14]One has to keep in mind, though, that foreign IPOs are typically more underpriced than domestic ones, an observation that appears to be mainly due to the fact that information asymmetries are more pronounced in such settings. Of course, higher underpricing means lower returns for the sellers, i.e., the firms going public and their partners, including the venture capitalists. See Francis et al. (2001) and Rock (2001) for a thorough discussion.

In addition to the scholarly debate, the views held by practitioners should not go unmentioned, either. The BVK (2005) has published a survey on German private equity companies' views of the importance of IPOs and stock markets more generally. While this survey does not tell us all that much about how IPOs influence fundraising activity directly – a survey of the perceived importance of IPOs among investors would be needed for this –, it nevertheless allows us a glimpse at how well founded in reality the academic discussion of the relevance of IPOs is. After all, if all practitioners agreed across the board that IPOs do not matter, then one would be hard pressed to dismiss such a fact based solely on insights from financial theory.

One interesting result of the BVK's survey of 106 private equity firms, which is evenly split between those focusing on early-stage financing (53) and those who primarily engage in later-stage activity (53), is that 51 of them reckon that the IPO market is very important for the German private equity market overall and 36 still regard it as important, while none think that it does not matter at all and only 2 that it matters little. When it comes to their own firm, these figures drop to 20 and 23 who attach (very) high importance to IPOs, while now 9 companies claim that they play no role whatsoever and 11 that they only matter a little.[15] Interestingly, early-stage financiers deem an active IPO market more important than companies focusing on later-stage activity. On a descending scale from 1 to 6, the former assign an average importance of 1.5 (2.5) for the market overall (the own company) to IPOs vs. 2.1 (3.5) for the latter group. Overall, 52 of the 106 private equity firms identified a total of 108 potential IPO candidates in their portfolios, 20 (39) of which are in the midst of preparing for an IPO in 2005 (2006).

Finally, the study also shows that German private equity firms rely quite extensively on foreign exchanges for listing their companies. While 82 firms stated that a domestic IPO was desirable, the option to have a portfolio company go public abroad was mentioned by 71 survey participants.[16] In-

[15]The ones who attach little or no importance to IPOs for their own companies are mainly small private equity funds attached to savings & loans institutes ("Sparkassen").

[16]Multiple answers regarding preferred IPO venues were possible.

terestingly, the UK's Alternative Investment Market (AIM) was named as a potential IPO venue 26 times, and mostly seen as an especially desirable outlet by early-stage financiers. All in all, the BVK study reveals that German private equity firms are interested in divesting their portfolio companies via an IPO and do not shy away from doing so abroad if need be.

The most comprehensive empirical study of the exit strategies that German private equity firms pursue is the one by Paffenholz (2004), who has collected survey data for a sample of 112 firms. Not surprisingly, when it comes to the main goals of exits, private equity firms in Germany rank the maximization of proceeds highest by a considerable margin: 63.9 percent of all respondents stated that this was their primary aim. Surprisingly, 8.3 percent of all respondents said that they do not aim at all to maximize their proceeds during an exit. These funds are typically subsidiaries of publicly-held banks, such as the *Sparkassen* and *Landesbanken*.[17]

One of the outstanding results reported by Paffenholz (2004) is certainly that the publicly-backed banks are most keen on selling their portfolio firms to the public, followed by corporate venture capitalists. Independent private equity firms, by contrast, prefer trade sales to IPOs, an attitude echoed by the German market overall.[18] Secondary purchases and share buy-backs, in turn, are uniformly regarded to be much less desirable than trade sales and stock market exits.

Overall, the actual attitude that is reflected in these results reinforces the notion that IPOs are not all-important in the venture capital cycle. Rather, the normally less spectacular trade sales play a role that is at least as important in the perception of private equity managers. Unfortunately, this relatively straightforward insight has not received due attention in the scholarly literature so far. The econometric analysis presented below therefore aims to mitigate the bias in favor of IPOs somewhat and explicitly includes the volume of proceeds from trade sales in the regression analysis.

---

[17] Paffenholz (2004: 158; 159, table 9)
[18] Paffenholz (2004: 164, table 12)

Regaining control

Perhaps the most-widely cited paper on the link between IPO activity and venture capital is the one by Black and Gilson (1998), which moreover refers to the U.S. and Germany repeatedly. The main idea of this paper is that an entrepreneur stands to regain control over his or her firm during an IPO, as contrasted to losing it more or less completely in the case of an acquisition. In other words, the authors set out to

> "explain the importance of the form of exit: why the potential for the venture capital provider to exit from a successful start-up *through an IPO*, available only through a stock market, allows venture capital providers to enter into implicit contracts with entrepreneurs concerning future control of startup firms, in a way not available in a bank-centered capital market. Thus, we make explicit a functional link between private and public equity markets: The implicit contract over future control that is permitted by the availability of exit through an IPO helps to explain the greater success of venture capital as an organizational form in stock market-centered systems."[19]

Without doubt, this is an interesting angle. However, their whole paper critically hinges on an argument that is not at all convincing. Before going into the details, however, let us quickly review the evidence Black and Gilson present. In their table 2 on page 249 they report the "correlation between venture capital backed IPOs and new capital commitments to venture capital funds," using U.S. data for 1978-1996. In principle, these results should resemble the ones by Gompers and Lerner discussed above, even though Black and Gilson for some reason just use the number of IPOs in the previous year instead of their total volume as the independent variable, but as a matter of fact, they do not – not even distantly.

[19]Black and Gilson (1998: 245, emphasis in original)

Table 6.2
Update of Black & Gilson's (1998) fundraising analysis

Independent variable	Estimate	Std. Error	*t*-value	Pr(>|t|)
(Intercept)	218.72	10143.77	0.0216	0.983
no. of US VC-IPOs at (t-1)	126.83	110.32	1.1497	0.263

Note: All standard errors are 'HC3' heteroscedasticity-adjusted.
The dependent variable is the amount of venture capital raised in USD.

To shed some light on the causes of this disagreement, I have replicated the analysis by Black and Gilson with the data for 1979 to 2003 that is reported in the latest NVCA Yearbook (2004), and the results are reported in table 6.2. What I found is that the regression result confirms Gompers and Lerner's findings. Based on this simple model, no effect of venture capital-related IPO activity on venture capital fundraising levels can be discerned in the data. As reported in the next section, this result holds true for other, more sophisticated specifications, too.

Upon close scrutiny, one crucial part of Black and Gilson's paper is even less convincing than their regression results:

> "Our IPO exit model requires three noncontroversial assumptions: (i) the entrepreneur places substantial private value on control over the company she starts; (ii) it is not feasible for an untested entrepreneur to retain control at the time of the initial venture capital financing; and (iii) it is feasible for a successful entrepreneur to reacquire control from the venture capitalist when the venture capitalist exits."[20]

So far, so good. However, shortly afterwards a passage that appears very problematic, to say the least, follows. It is repeated here in its entirety, and it is meant by Black and Gilson to convince the reader of the validity of claim (i) quoted above:

[20] Black and Gilson (1998: 258)

> "A private value for control is a standard feature in venture capital models and, more generally, in models that seek to explain the incentive properties of capital structure [...]. Moreover, for entrepreneurs, the assumption appears to be descriptively accurate. The failure rate for startup companies is high enough so that, without a large private value for control, many potential entrepreneurs would decide not to leave a job to start a new company. It is also apparent that ceding to the venture capital provider the power, frequently exercised, to remove the entrepreneur from management is a significant cost to the entrepreneur."[21]

If one pays close attention, it is difficult to see how the last sentence could strengthen Black and Gilson's argument, as it appears to express just the opposite of conjecture (i): entrepreneurs seek venture capital funding *despite* a good chance that they will be ousted by the venture capitalists at one point in time notwithstanding their assumed unwillingness to leave the start-up. Yet more irritatingly, how does this point fit together with (ii)? The entrepreneur does not have the means to continue funding the venture on her own, so she has to go to a venture capitalist. At the same time, she "places substantial private value on control over the company she starts." If I read this correctly, she is left with no choice but to go to the venture capitalist, anyways (which follows from (ii)).[22]

Yet, in a market where there are no IPOs, because of (i) an entrepreneur would presumably walk away from a deal such as the $6.9 billion Cerent trade sale mentioned earlier, just because it is nearly impossible (safe for a highly unlikely share buyback) to regain control over the start-up? In other words, when faced with the choice between cashing out during an acquisition

[21] Black and Gilson (1998: 258-259)

[22] Florin (2005) argues that empirically those founders who wish to remain at the helm of their firm should refrain from seeking venture capitalist involvement, further indicating that often there is simply no choice for the entrepreneur but to seek this form of outside financing.

and simply not doing anything, most if not all (potential) entrepreneurs will choose the latter? Upon careful examination of the causal logic, it indeed appears doubtful that this view is "noncontroversial," as Black and Gilson would have it.

On a related note, how influential Black and Gilson's 1998 paper unfortunately is in the German literature can be seen from a quote from Franzke et al. (2003: 18), who have tried to (qualitatively) analyze why there are relatively few IPOs and venture capital funds in Germany: "Black and Gilson (1998) argue that a well-functioning stock market with an active IPO market is a prerequisite for an active VC market. In this case what needs to be analyzed can be reduced to the question why there are so few IPOs." Yet, as was argued above, such a view is misleading, as simply no causal link between IPOs and venture capital activity can be found in the data.

Grandstanding

Last but not least, there is the idea that IPOs are important simply because they allow young venture capital funds to signal their quality to potential investors. For the U.S., this view is both theoretically well grounded and backed by good empirical observations, but it is not entirely clear how it transfers from the U.S. to Germany.[23]

The seminal paper on the grandstanding phenomenon is Gompers (1996), and it summarizes the main argument as follows:

> "I develop and test the hypothesis that young venture capital firms take companies public earlier than older venture capital firms in order to establish a reputation and successfully raise capital for new funds [this behavior is referred to as "grandstanding"]. Evidence from a sample of 433 IPOs suggests that companies backed by young venture capital firms are younger and more underpriced at their IPO than those of established venture cap-

[23]See Cumming et al. (2005) for an interesting discussion of some empirical evidence on venture capital firm characteristics and fundraising.

> ital firms. Moreover, young venture capital firms have been on the board of directors a shorter period of time at the IPO, hold smaller equity stakes, and time the IPO to precede or coincide with raising money for follow-on funds."[24]

The paper by Gompers (1996) relies on two extensive samples, one that covers 433 venture capital-backed IPOs from the beginning of 1978 through year-end 1987, and a second one that includes the first IPO that 62 venture capital funds undertook during the same period. A more recent empirical investigation by Lee and Wahal (2004) reaches essentially the same verdict based on a sample of 6,413 IPOs that took pace between 1980 and 2000, and overall the grandstanding argument appears to rest on a very firm empirical foundation at least in the case of the U.S. market.

Hyytinen (2005) uses 2001 survey data from Finland to gauge how much importance a comprehensive sample of 39 Finnish venture capital firms attributes to stock market exits. Overall, his data set reveals that especially the younger venture capital firms tend to be concerned about IPO options already during the early stages of the venture capital cycle and deem them important for follow-on fundraising. Based on this fact and two other arguments, Hyytinen (2005: 144) subsequently concludes that "[t]hese three pieces of evidence support the view that the codevelopment of the market for exits is likely to be instrumental for the long-term development of the Finnish venture capital industry."

However, his conclusion is not convincing, as he fails to provide any evidence that investors value proceeds (of the same volume) from an IPO more than those from a trade sale or that the proceeds from an IPO are higher than those for a trade sale for the same portfolio company. Absent such evidence, his observation amounts to not much more than a restatement of the well-known selection effects that one would expect to find here, as discussed above. To reiterate: It is likely that portfolio firms that have been taken public via an IPO are simply more valuable than those that are sold in a

---

[24] Gompers (1996: 133)

trade sale. The observation that an IPO took place thus only reflects the underlying quality of the portfolio firm, but in no way shows that the IPO in and of itself made the investment more successful. Finding such an "IPO premium" should prove difficult, though, as the financial economics literature generally agrees that there typically is an "IPO discount," i.e., firms are offered to the public at a price that can lie 10 or more percent below their fair value (NPV), and is likely to be even greater under grandstanding. Why potential investors in venture capital funds should welcome such a discount, though, remains entirely unclear from Hyytinen's (2005) paper.

A potential implication of the grandstanding phenomenon is the need for the many young German venture capitalists to accept lower returns for the time being, just to be able to take a company public and to thereby signal their quality to potential investors in a follow-on fund. On average, this would of course depress returns in the German venture capital market relative to the more mature U.S. market, and by extension the younger market would automatically be smaller.

However, as the survey results reported by Paffenholz (2004: 157, table 8) show, only 8.3 percent of the 112 firms in his sample consider "improving the track record" as their primary goal during an exit. By contrast, 13.9 percent of all private equity firms claim to not pursue this goal at all, which in turn renders grandstanding pointless. Once more, the firms that care least about their track record are those affiliated with publicly-held *Sparkassen* and *Landesbanken*, while independent firms value this aspect more highly, only to be outdone by corporate venture capitalists.[25]

In addition, as there are relatively few well-established players in Germany that younger firms compete with during the fundraising stage, anyways, it is not immediately clear that new venture capitalists will have to signal their quality via an (early) IPO of a portfolio company. After all, they are probably not competing as much against already entrenched players as new venture capital firms in the U.S. are.

[25]Paffenholz (2004: 159, table 9)

6.2 New evidence on the link between IPOs and venture capital

6.2.1 Approach

Against the background of the theoretical discussion above, this section takes a look at the empirical record. The main goal is to check whether one can find evidence for the relevance of those factors that are usually said to be the actual determinants of fundraising activity in the U.S. and Germany. Three sets of regression models, which are grouped according to the dependent variable, are presented. The dependent variables are the commitments of venture capital in the U.S. (model 1), the commitments of private equity in the U.S. (model 2), and the commitments of private equity in Germany (model 3). Later on, a time-series analysis of these variables follows. Before presenting the results, however, a discussion of the manifold problems an empirical investigation is faced with is in order.

The major problem – and one that cannot be overcome – is that the number of observations is generally very small, simply because the modern venture capital industry is still young. The available number of observations ranges from 19-21 data points for the U.S. to only 11-13 observations in the case of the German market, where data on private equity-backed M&A activity is only available from 1992 onwards.

A different objection to the ordinary least-squares (OLS) regression below that some might raise is that we are almost certainly faced with a time trend in all data series. GDP in current prices, the three stock market indices, and the venture capital and private equity figures all increase with time. Despite occasional setbacks, already at first glance their mean exhibits a notable upward trend.[26] Yet, given the limited number of observations that are available and for comparability with other studies, I have decided to disregard the time trends in a first step of the analysis and to use a simple

[26] This impression is confirmed by the time-series analysis below.

OLS framework without a time-trend correction to analyze possible effects of several independent variables on fundraising activity.

Having said this, a somewhat more sophisticated time-series analysis is carried out, too, yet given the data limitations problematic. Above all, the "spikes" in fundraising activity in the years 1998 to 2001 – and here especially in 1999 and 2000 – render a sensible analysis difficult. I thus limit the time-series analysis to a (univariate) discussion of the properties of the dependent variables. More exactly, I try to find a good characterization of the series as stationary ARIMA processes and later on use the preferred specification as the basis for a ten-year forecast. The results presented should make clear which formidable obstacles have to be overcome by the analyst, and I hope that other researchers will fill the need for more sophisticated analysis at some point.[27]

6.2.2 OLS analysis

This section presents the results of an OLS analysis of fundraising activity.[28] Information on the dependent and independent variables is presented in various tables that show the respective regression output, and the natural logarithm of several variables was used so that increases and decreases in the variables are treated symmetrically. As there is ample reason to suspect that heteroscedasticity (of unknown form) is present in the data, I have throughout computed standard errors based on a heteroscedasticity-consistent covariance matrix (HCCM). Following the advice given by Long and Ervin (2000), I choose the 'HC3' algorithm, which in small samples performs better than the widely used 'HC0' estimator. Moreover, even if a formal test does not reveal the presence of heteroscedasticity, the 'HC3' correction is used nevertheless, as there is no good theoretical reason to expect a constant error-variance.

[27] One promising approach is to use quarterly or even monthly data to increase the number of data points. Yet, such information was not available to me except for the most recent years.

[28] All computations were performed in R 2.1.0.

In addition to the heteroscedasticity correction, all standard diagnostic tests have been performed.[29] Surprisingly, relatively few problems have been discovered. The presence of influential observations is less frequent than the small samples and at times large jumps in the data might lead one to expect. When potentially influential observations—those with high standardized *df-beta* or *Cook's D* values—are present, however, an additional regression that excludes such observations is run as a form of "robustness check."

A final set of caveats is in order here. The OLS analysis below rests on the assumption that the values used are normally distributed. This, however, is quite likely not the case. In most financial markets, one has to deal with "fat tails," i.e., more observations fall into the tails of the distribution than is the case for a normal distribution. Techniques other than OLS, such as non-parametric approaches, should ideally be used in a setting such as this so that no *a priori* assumptions about the distribution of the data, its functional form, and the error terms have to be made, yet the small sample size (recall: $11 \leq n \leq 21$) renders such an approach infeasible. I hope that the reader will agree, however, that a careful—albeit tentative—analysis such as the one presented below is worth carrying out if the best alternative is to wait another 20 or so years until "enough" data has accumulated.

The U.S. market

Table 6.3 shows that we cannot exclude the possibility that the venture capital-backed IPO volume in the current year does *not* have any effect on the volume of venture capital raised in the U.S. when NASDAQ performance and venture capital-backed M&A activity are taken into account at the same time.[30] The latter, by contrast, has a clear positive effect on fundraising activity, as theoretical considerations would lead one to suspect. The coefficient for venture capital-backed M&A activity is approximately 0.48 in model

[29]Chapters 2 and 3 in Belsley et al. (1980) give a comprehensive overview of the most important diagnostic tests.

[30]Both NASDAQ and Dow Jones performance were included as control variables to—at least crudely—measure and reflect the stock market sentiment in a given year.

Table 6.3
Determinants of U.S. venture capital and private equity fundraising levels

Independent variable	Model 1 a†	Model 1 b†	Model 2 a‡	Model 2 b‡
Natural log of U.S. VC-IPO volume	0.0603 (0.2589)	—	−0.0447 (0.1611)	—
Natural log of U.S. VC-IPO volume in the previous year	—	−0.0195 (0.3534)	—	0.1403 (0.2305)
Natural log of U.S. VC-M&A volume	0.4761** (0.1084)	0.5010* (0.1871)	—	—
Natural log of U.S. PE-M&A volume	—	—	0.5276** (0.0794)	0.4679** (0.0644)
NASDAQ performance	−0.0011 (0.0068)	−0.0010 (0.0077)	—	—
Dow Jones performance	—	—	0.0000 (0.0086)	0.0017 (0.0106)
N	19	19	21	21

† dependent variable: natural logarithm of venture capital commitments
‡ dependent variable: natural logarithm of private equity commitments
Note: Standard errors, which are all computed using the 'HC3' heteroscedasticity-adjustment, are shown in parentheses. All regressions include an (unreported) constant. Significance levels are denoted as follows: ◇: $p < 0.10$, *: $p < 0.05$, **: $p < 0.01$.

1(a), indicating that a one percent increase in M&A activity is expected to on average lead to a 0.48 percentage point increase in fundraising volume.[31]

Very similar results are obtained when the IPO volume is lagged by a year (model 1(b)), so that the IPO volume in the previous year helps determine commitments in the current year. It has been suggested in the literature that IPOs send a strong signal to potential investors, but as the fundraising process is prone to some (often administrative and legal) delays, inflows will only be recorded with a lag of at least several months. However, no solid

[31] Regression diagnostics reveal that, for model 1(a), the observation for the year 2000 potentially influences the regression results, while in the case of model 2(b) the year 1981 might influence the results—high values for both the standardized *dfbetas* and *Cook's D* are found in each case. Re-running the regression with these observations excluded yields essentially the same findings, however, so that only those results obtained for the complete samples are reported here.

evidence—meaning that the coefficient for the lagged variable is expected to be different from zero with a probability of at least 90%—can be found for the validity of this alternative model about the importance of IPOs, either.

When trying to identify what drives fundraising for the broader private equity category, a picture very similar to that for venture capital emerges. As reported in table 6.3, based on the models 2(a) and 2(b), one finds that only the level of private equity-backed M&A activity exerts a statistically significant influence on new commitments.[32] Once more, given the coefficient for M&A activity of approximately 0.50 and the logarithmic presentation of the data, we would expect a one percent increase in M&A activity to on average lead to a 0.50 percentage point increase in fundraising activity.

The results obtained here match those reported by Gompers & Lerner (1998) strikingly well. As noted in chapter 6.1, they likewise assert that fundraising activity from 1972-1994 is not influenced by the previous year's IPO volume when averaging across all groups of investors.[33] These findings are echoed by the more recent data used here, too. All in all, the NVCA data for the years 1984 to 2004 that was used as the basis for the OLS regressions presented above does not allow one to conclude that IPO activity and venture capital fundraising are closely linked. The fact that many earlier papers have argued for (and reported) such a connection seems to be at least in part attributable to the fact that homoskedasticity of the error terms has often simply been assumed rather than shown to exist in the data and that important control variables, first and foremost the level of venture capital- or private equity-backed M&A activity, have been omitted.

The German market

Data availability for Germany is an even bigger problem than in the case of the U.S., and one should keep in mind that the results presented below

[32]Unfortunately, the NVCA does not provide data on the private equity-backed IPO volume, so that the (natural logarithm of the) venture capital-backed IPO volume is included in the regressions instead.

[33]See especially Gompers & Lerner (1998: 166, table 2).

Table 6.4
Determinants of German private equity fundraising levels

Independent variable	Model 3 a† (all years)	Model 3 a'† (excl. 1997)	Model 3 b†
Natural log of German PE-IPO volume	0.6670 (0.7832)	1.3892** (0.3999)	—
Natural log of German PE-IPO volume in the previous year	—	—	0.8610 (0.4681)
Natural log of German PE-M&A volume	0.8073 (1.0970)	−0.0449 (0.9064)	1.4366* (0.4208)
DAX performance	0.0041 (0.0163)	-0.0054 (0.0177)	0.0206* (0.0063)
N	13	12	11

† dependent variable: natural logarithm of private equity commitments

Note: Standard errors, which are all computed using the 'HC3' heteroscedasticity-adjustment, are shown in parentheses. All regressions include an (unreported) constant. Significance levels are denoted as follows: ⋄: $p < 0.10$, *: $p < 0.05$, **: $p < 0.01$.

have to be interpreted with strong caution. At best, (only) 13 observations are available (for the years 1992 to 2004), which is certainly a lower limit for a valid OLS analysis.[34] Even worse, fundraising data for venture capital is only available from 1999 on, and I have thus decided not to carry out any statistical analysis based on these 6 observations for the years 1999 to 2004. As year-end comparisons are problematic due to membership changes in the BVK, the data used here is intra-year data and thus expresses the fundraising volume from January 1 to December 31 of a given year. This ensures that no exogenous shocks that solely stem from a changing BVK membership roster are reflected in the results.[35] A complete description of the data used in this analysis along with its sources can be found in the data appendix.

[34]The most common rule of thumb is that 30 observations or more should be used, as in that case one can assume with some confidence that the limit theorems used in OLS analysis hold. The exact number required for a correct analysis can be lower or higher, though, ultimately depending on the underlying sample.

[35]Refer back to chapter 4.3 for an exhaustive discussion of this point.

As table 6.4 shows, unlike for the U.S., in the case of the German private equity market one finds no clear-cut results regarding the determinants of fundraising activity. Depending on the specification of the regression equation, one either finds that no independent variable seems to matter (model 3(a)), that private equity-backed IPO volume matters while private equity-backed M&A activity does not appear to exert an effect on private equity fundraising (model 3(a)′, which excludes the year 1997), or, finally, that both private equity-backed M&A activity and DAX performance help determine the level of fundraising activity, while one-year-lagged IPO volumes do not (model 3(b)).[36] The only impartial conclusion that one can draw for the German market is thus that an OLS analysis of the available data for the years 1993 to 2004 that is theoretically informed does not allow us to securely pinpoint a single domestic factor that would help predict private equity fundraising activity.

One final observation in this part of the analysis should be made. When running a regression that uses the natural logarithm of private equity fundraising activity in the U.S. as the sole independent variable to predict what will happen to its German counterpart, one obtains a statistically significant coefficient (coefficient: 0.9594; 'HC3'-corrected standard error: 0.2829). The German market thus appears to be "linked" to its American counterpart. In other words, the focus on domestic variables that is reflected in the regression equations above, as well as in the wider literature, might well be misleading. As has variously been noted, success stories, such as that of the Israeli venture capital market, can be found even in countries where IPO activity is low, as listing at a foreign exchange is still possible even if the domestic stock market lies dormant.[37] Exploring such international linkages lies beyond the scope of this book, however.

[36]1997 was identified as potentially influential in regression 3(a) using several diagnostic tests. Unlike in the earlier U.S. cases with potentially influential observations, re-running the regression with this data point excluded yields markedly different results.

[37]Gompers & Lerner (1998) argue in this vein, too.

6.2.3 Time-series analysis

The next paragraphs discuss the time-series properties of the data on U.S. venture capital commitments and on private equity fundraising in both the U.S. and Germany. I have tried to identify them based on the notion that they can be expressed as autoregressive integrated moving-average (ARIMA) processes and assuming that none of the parameters in the model are greater than 2.[38]

The plot for U.S. venture capital commitments strongly suggests that we are not dealing with a stationary series. In fact, only differencing twice gives us a stationary series, as the Augmented Dickey-Fuller (ADF) test shows. The plot of the auto-correlation function (ACF) and partial auto-correlation function (PACF) in figure 6.1 hints at an ARIMA(0,2,2) process, as the ACF ends abruptly after two spikes for lags 1 and 2, while the PACF "dampens down," i.e., gradually approaches zero over time, a pattern generally associated with MA(2) processes. The Akaike information criterion (AIC), however, reaches its lowest value for an ARIMA(0,2,1) specification, namely 548.37 vs. 550.02 for the ARIMA(0,2,2) model. Given the premium that is usually placed on parsimony, this leads me to conclude that the data on commitments to U.S. venture capital funds can best be described by a ARIMA(0,2,1) model.[39]

Next, I turn to the analysis of private equity commitments in the U.S. Again, it is necessary to difference the series twice to induce stationarity, as indicated by the ADF test. The pattern of the ACF and PACF in figure 6.2 is very similar to that for venture capital commitments, yet this time there is only one spike in the ACF, leading to the conclusion that we are dealing with an ARIMA(0,2,1) process. In this case, the AIC indeed achieves its lowest value for this specification, and this model is therefore chosen.

[38] Readers who are not familiar with basic time-series analysis should refer to Hamilton (1994) for more information.

[39] Diagnostics for this specification, such as a look at the ACF of the residuals and the p-values for the Ljung-Box statistic, confirm its appropriateness. This information can be obtained via the '`tsdiag()`' command in R 2.1 when the '`tseries`' library is loaded.

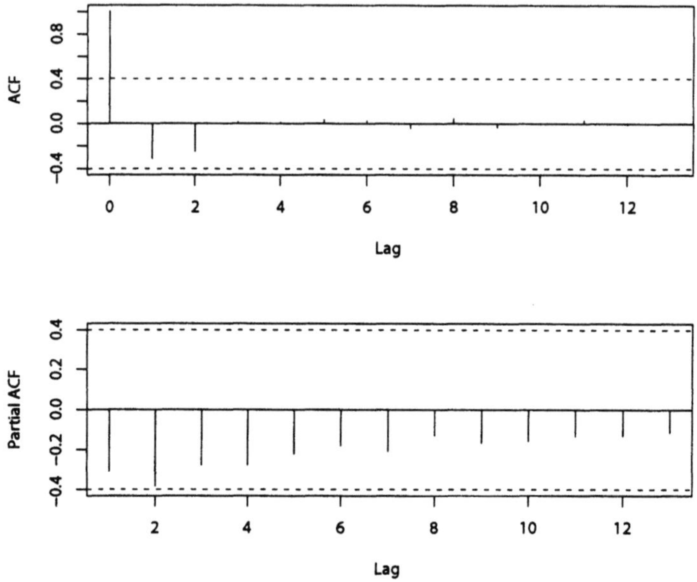

Figure 6.1
ACF and PACF plots for venture capital commitments in the U.S.

The final step is to identify the model that best describes the German private equity fundraising data. Once more, the ADF test shows that differencing the original data twice is required to induce stationarity. Unlike in the case of the U.S. data, however, the ACF and PACF in figure 6.3 leads one to assume that we are dealing with an ARIMA(1,2,0) process. Indeed, this time the lowest AIC value is obtained for an ARIMA(1,2,0) model, namely 246.45, which is slightly lower than the 250.22 reported for the ARIMA(0,2,1) specification. The diagnostics indicate that both specifications are valid, and the AR(1) coefficient reported is −0.8438, with a standard error of 0.1340.

Given the lower AIC value and the plots of the ACF and PACF that indicate an autoregressive process, I have decided to employ the ARIMA(1,2,0) model as my preferred specification for the German data. One should keep in mind, however, that the results for Germany are based on only 13 obser-

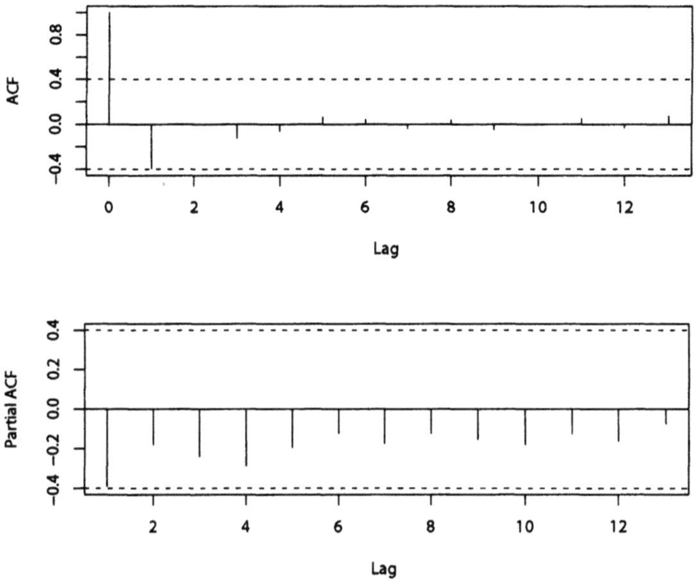

Figure 6.2
ACF and PACF plots for private equity commitments in the U.S.

vations, of which many are "problematic," i.e., they are for 1998-2002, which were especially turbulent years. As there is little theoretical reason to suspect that the processes in Germany and the U.S. differ, though, I used both specifications to predict German private equity fundraising levels 10 years into the future and the reader is of course welcome to draw a conclusion regarding the best model for the German data that differs from mine.

Based on the work presented above, I calculated the predicted values of venture capital and private equity commitments 10 years into the future. As can be seen from the figures 6.4 to 6.7, these predictions come with considerable margins of error, as the confidence intervals indicating $\pm$ 2 standard errors make clear (lines with dots). When using the ARIMA(0,2,1) setup, all commitment levels are predicted to increase over time. Only when the ARIMA(1,2,0) model for Germany is used are fundraising levels predicted to

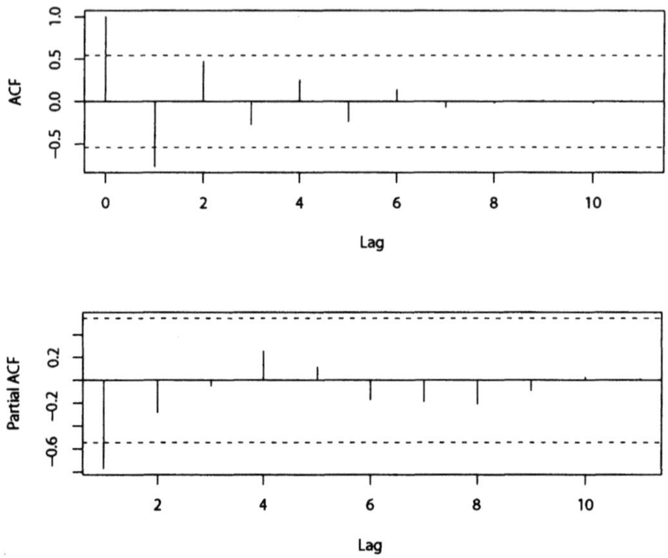

Figure 6.3
ACF and PACF plots for private equity commitments in Germany

fall below 0 by the year 2008 and to spiral downwards from then on, as can be seen in figure 6.6.

What should be clear by now is how difficult it is to generate a sound forecast for German private equity commitment levels. The OLS analysis already indicated that the determinants of fundraising activity are anything but clear in Germany, and the time-series analysis points in the same direction. If we take the results presented here seriously, then we have to believe that there will be no more funds flowing into the German private equity industry from 2008 on. However, such a conclusion is certainly misleading. All it shows is how difficult a sound empirical analysis of the German data still is, above all due to the short time span for which data is available.

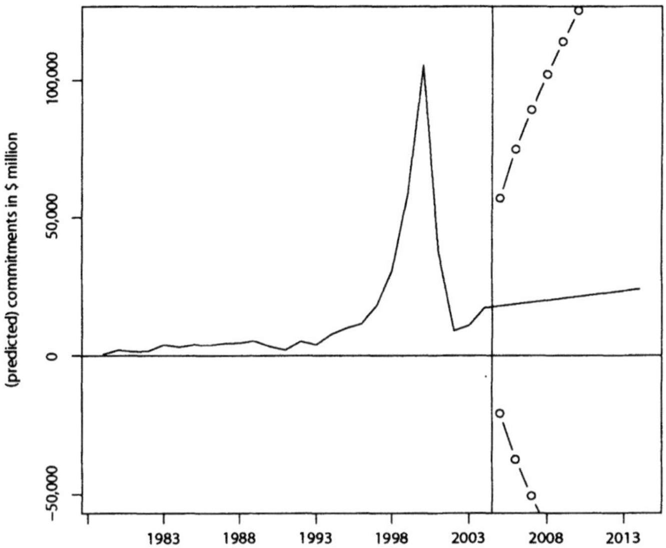

Figure 6.4
Actual and predicted venture capital commitments in the U.S.

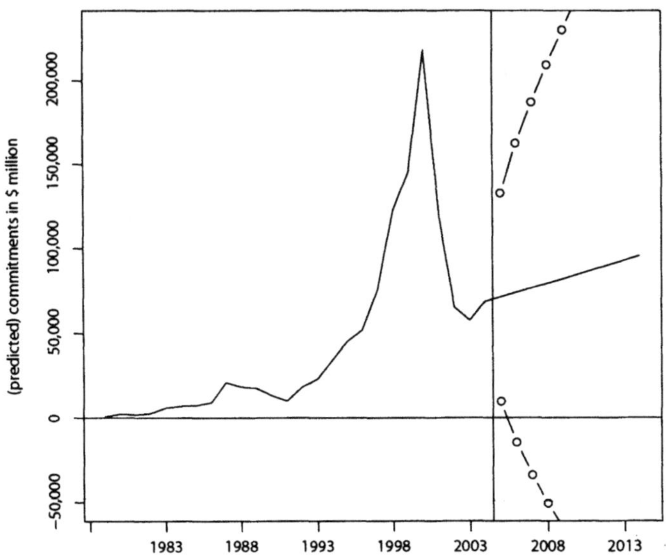

Figure 6.5
Actual and predicted private equity commitments in the U.S.

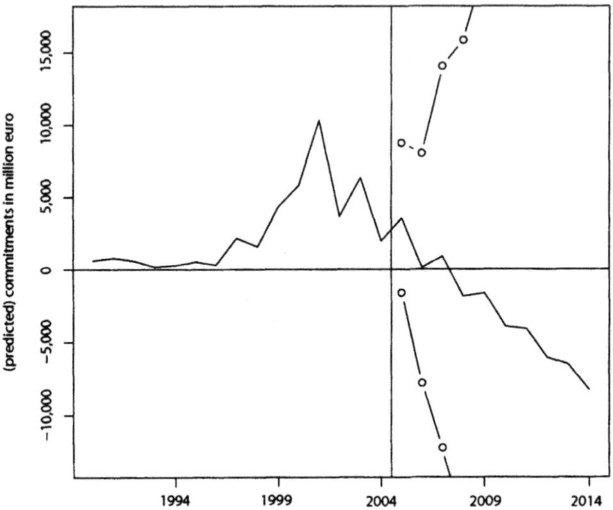

Figure 6.6
Actual and predicted private equity commitments in Germany based on the preferred ARIMA(1,2,0) specification

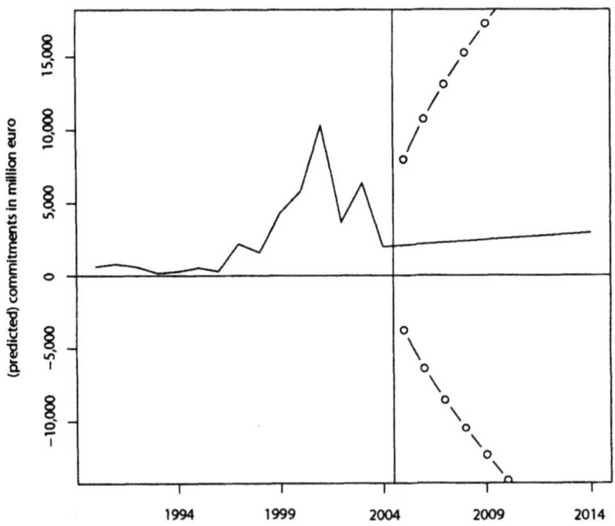

Figure 6.7
Actual and predicted private equity commitments in Germany based on the alternative ARIMA(0,2,1) specification

Chapter 7

Supply and demand in perspective

The question whether supply or demand is holding back the growth of the venture capital market is not new.[1] However, for Germany it has not been contemplated seriously in the literature so far. In terms of the design of an effective public policy aimed at fostering venture capital activity, this is most unfortunate. After all, if we do not even know where the bottleneck lies, how can we design policies to help widen it, other than by relying on pure luck? Even more troubling, it appears that public policy for venture capital has been seriously and systematically misguided in the past. As was laid out in chapter 4.4, all governmental initiatives have so far by and large met with little, if any, success. It is little comfort, then, that similar schemes have not yielded the envisioned positive results on the other side of the Atlantic, either: "In the United States, programs like the Department of Commerce's Advanced Technology Program (ATP) have disbursed over $1 billion to small high-technology businesses over the past ten years, with few tangible results."[2]

[1] See for example Gompers and Lerner (1998c) for an extensive overview of such a discussion for the U.S.

[2] Gompers and Lerner (2001a: 16)

It is striking that public policy seems to be beset by systematic problems. Even with a random design, at least a few of the several hundred programs in Germany and the U.S. should be successful, even if just by chance. However, I contend in the following that the universal lack of success of these programs has its root in the fact that the supply of venture capital has been targeted predominantly, while indeed insufficient demand is holding back the growth of the market, leading to systematic failure of all public programs. How fixated on supply-side problems not only those who design public policy, but also researchers are, becomes clear by a look at a study by Albach and Köster (1997). While they dedicate roughly one page to the enumeration of six reasons that might lead to a lack of demand for venture capital in Germany, none of which is the simple lack of *qualified* demand, they dedicate six pages to listing a whopping 31 potential supply-side constraints.[3]

In order to substantiate my claim of lack of demand, I first review the strongest arguments put forward in favor of the lack-of-supply hypothesis. I conclude that most of these rest on shaky foundations both theoretically and empirically. Rather than discussing demand-side factors at length, which would include such fuzzy concepts as the general business climate, relative risk aversion, labor market rigidities, and lack of entrepreneurial spirit in Germany – all topics whose thorough treatment would be far beyond what can be covered in a short book such as this –, I instead logically infer that if supply is not the bottleneck, then it must be demand. To some, this may seem a daring inference. In response to such doubts, I review the pertinent literature on public policy programs for venture capital in the final part of this chapter, which, as it turns out, is by and large in line with my reasoning.

It should not go unmentioned, however, that in reality there is a feedback loop present that resembles a chicken-and-egg problem. As Roling (2001) shows in his econometric study, increased venture capital activity stimulates innovations and patenting, while at the same time high rates of innovations and patenting are conducive to more venture capital investing.[4]

[3]Albach and Köster (1997: 17-23)

[4]Roling (2001: 111) uses a Granger causality test to establish this relationship.

7.1 Supply bottlenecks

Three supply-side stories are routinely brought up when the relative lack of venture capital in Germany is discussed.[5] First, the lack of an active stock market segment in Germany comparable to the NASDAQ has received considerable attention. Even though the now defunct *Neuer Markt* provided such an outlet from 1997 to 2002, the overall lesser stock market orientation of the German financial system is often seen as a barrier on the road to more venture capital activity, as placing lucrative initial public offerings (IPOs) is simply more difficult, thus depressing returns.[6] This argument has already been discussed at length in the previous chapter, and the conclusion of the discussion there is that the often conjectured dependence of the venture capital market on IPOs and thus an active stock market does not exist.

Second, many see high German tax rates on capital gains as hindering the expansion of venture capital.[7] Finally, the fact that pension funds, the most active investors in venture capital funds, do not exist in Germany to an extent comparable to the U.S. or the UK is at times also blamed for limited supply. I will consider these arguments in turn, without going into too much detail, however.

In an interesting paper, Schmidt (1988) summarizes his experience with German venture capital managers. Based on a survey sent out to the managers of venture capital firms, he found that they consider the restrictive investment guidelines applying to insurance companies and the lack of pension funds in Germany as the main obstacle on the way towards a more vigorous venture capital market in Germany. This point is closely followed by complaints about the tax code and lack of access to the stock market, which both render the "VC climate" in Germany much less favorable than in the U.S. and Great Britain. However, as Schmidt (1988) repeatedly points out, none of these views hold up to a reality check. Especially troubling

[5]This chapter will only refer to the situation in the U.S. when it is especially illuminating. Otherwise, the focus is solely on Germany.

[6]See Güllmann (2000: 250-256) for an institutional overview.

[7]This argument has variously been applied to demand, too; see chapter 7.2 below.

is the fact that only one manager out of at least a dozen showed at least a basic understanding of the German tax code, while not a single manager even claimed to know which differences exist between the IPO regulations in Germany and other countries.

Taxation and sources of funds

The German tax system is notoriously complex.[8] Literally thousands of rules and regulations exist, and it is often not even clear which rules apply to whom when. Instead of laying out all provisions that might prove relevant in the context of venture capital financing – again a task which lies beyond what can be accomplished in a book such as this –, I will provide a review of the central literature that exists on this issue. Most of it abstracts from concrete passages of the German tax code, which would at a minimum include the *Körperschafts-*, *Gewerbeertrags-*, *Einkommen-* and *Grundsteuer* as well as the *Solidaritätszuschlag*, and focuses instead on the overall effects of taxation.[9]

"Few economic problems are currently of more direct concern to the American citizen or to the American business firm than the present tax structure and the tax structure of the immediate future," Abbott and Zuckert (1941: 667) already observed more than half a century ago. Not much has changed since then on both sides of the Atlantic, one might argue. Surprisingly, then, this interest is not reflected in the literature on venture capital. Very few papers, among them Gompers and Lerner (1998c) and Poterba (1989), have investigated the potential effects of changes in tax rates on the U.S. venture capital industry, and to my knowledge to date no comparable study exists for Germany.

[8] I refrain here from discussing both the U.S. tax system and the effects taxation has on the structure of individual venture capital funds and single venture capital deals. See Rosen (1999) for an introduction to the former and Gilson and Schizer (2003) on the latter.

[9] For a more detailed review of the legal intricacies, the interested reader is referred to Güllmann (2000: 205-239), Nevermann and Falk (1986: 121-138), and Watrin and Gocksch (2002).

Poterba (1989: i) concludes after a thorough review of the evidence for 1969 to 1988:

> "The supply of funds is unlikely to be the principal mechanism through which the [capital gains] tax affects venture capital, since less than half of venture investors face individual capital gains tax liability on their realized gains. Moreover, most of the growth in venture funding during the last decade has come from tax-exempt investors."

Likewise, Gompers and Lerner (1998c: 167, emphasis added) assert:

> "Although we do find an effect of capital gains taxes on venture capital commitments, it does not appear to be working through the supply side. If changes in the capital gains tax rates had a first-order effect on investors' willingness to invest in venture capital, the effect would be strongest for individuals and taxable parties. *The opposite is true.*"

Does this mean that tax rates have no major influence on the supply of venture capital in Germany, either? Potentially it does, but such a conclusion would probably underestimate the effect that lower tax rates can have on the behavior of German investors. Another alternative asset, stakes in commercial ships (*Schiffsbeteiligungen*), is a case in point. As Lloyd Fonds AG (2003: 1) reports, this form of tax-favored investment is remarkably popular in Germany. In 1996, close to €4 billion were invested in funds that market stakes in commercial ships, and in 2002 this figure stood at a still respectable €1.4 billion. Strikingly, these investment volumes – nearly exclusively contributed by wealthy individuals seeking to avoid taxation – dwarf the commitments to the private equity industry in Germany by a factor of 12 for 1996 and those to venture capital funds by a factor of 1.38 for 2002.

Table 7.1
Sources of private equity commitments in Germany according to geographic origin, 1999-2004

	1999	2000	2001	2002	2003	2004
funds raised in Germany	53.88%	79.26%	34.10%	40.50%	17.90%	80.80%
...in the rest of Europe	27.55%	10.07%	37.30%	15.30%	41.20%	6.90%
...outside Europe	16.37%	9.92%	28.60%	44.20%	40.90%	12.40%

Source: BVK Statistik, various years.

The potential impact of changes in taxation on the supply of funds should therefore not be underestimated and might even outweigh the effects of all formal programs aimed at nurturing venture capital activity taken together. If undersupply were really a problem, the best solution would thus probably be to simply tax-exempt all investors in venture capital funds from capital gains taxes.

The comparison with fund inflows to funds for *Schiffsbeteiligungen* is admittedly only indicative, but it shows that Germany certainly does not lack sufficient overall savings to sustain an active venture capital market.[10] It also appears unlikely that the supply of funds could be a binding constraint on the venture capital industry in the U.S. Recently the decision of one of the oldest Silicon Valley venture capital firms, Sequoia Capital, to oust several academic institutions from its funds, has generated some headlines.[11] Sequoia can apparently afford such behavior, which means that other investors must be ready to replace the University of Michigan and the University of California as providers of investment money. Finally, recently there have been large inflows of funds into the German private equity industry from abroad, as table 7.1 makes clear, further undermining the notion that insufficient supply of capital by German investors hinders the development of the domestic private equity market.

[10] On a related note, two recent papers by van Osnabrugge and Robinson (2001) and Mayer et al. (2005) investigate how their sources of funds may influence the behavior of venture capital firms. Both articles find that the behavior of venture capitalists is influenced somewhat by whom they receive their money from.

[11] See for instance the article by Shinal (2003) in the San Francisco Chronicle.

The German government has recently – once more – tried to redesign the tax code to make it more friendly for private equity investors.[12] The changes include a December 2003 guideline called "BMF-Schreiben zur Fondsbesteuerung, den Carried Interest-Altfällen und der Umsatzsteuer auf Management Fees" as well as a new July 2004 law ("Gesetz zur Förderung von Wagniskapital") that applies to new carried-interest cases.[13] The BVK (2004b) surveyed the German private equity scene on its views about these new regulations and found that out of 52 firms, 6 regarded these changes as important and beneficial to their fundraising process, 23 considered them as at least somewhat important, and another 23 stated that they are irrelevant in this regard. Out of 102 firms, 68 consider recent tax code changes as beneficial to the overall fundraising situation in Germany, 28 expect no effect, and 6 even regard the recent reforms as detrimental.[14]

7.2 Demand factors

As stated at the outset of this chapter, I regard the apparent absence of lack of supply, both visible in the data presented in chapter 5 and backed by the preceding refutation of the generally strongest arguments in favor of supply constraints, as a strong indicator in favor of the lack-of-demand view expressed earlier. Nevertheless, before turning to the discussion of the pertinent literature on public policy for venture capital, some effects of taxation on demand are outlined, and a comparative overview of the "cost of entry" in the U.S. and Germany is provided.

A succinct discussion of the unfavorable entrepreneurial climate in Germany especially in the early days of the German venture capital industry is provided by Becker and Hellmann (2005: 55-59). The overall picture that

[12]The first such efforts can be traced back to at least 1986, when the "Gesetz über Unternehmensbeteiligungsgesellschaften" was passed. See Frommann (1993: 25-26) for a discussion of the law's provisions and its shortcomings.

[13]BVK (2004b: 6)

[14]Watrin and Gocksch (2002) also deem many of these reforms problematic.

they sketch of the demand side in the 1970s and 1980s is nothing short of devastating and certainly helps explain the relative backwardness of the German venture capital market when compared to the U.S. to a good extent.

Taxation

It is certainly fair to say that no one enjoys paying high taxes, and that nearly all forms of taxation are distortionary is a well-known result from the public finance literature, a fact normally referred to under the heading "excess burden." However, high marginal tax rates also mean that potential tax credits for investment are high, favoring investment over consumption. Moreover, especially in the context of small business finance, taxation does not necessarily only represent a burden. As most firms which receive venture capital-backing are unprofitable, anyways, high marginal tax rates should be of relatively little immediate concern to them. Moreover, as Bulow and Summers (1984) have argued, in high-risk environments, high marginal tax rates tend to make investments less risky for an investor. In a similar vein, Gordon (1985: 1) argues:

> "[W]hen uncertainty is taken into account explicitly, taxation of corporate income can leave corporate investment incentives, and individual savings incentives, basically unaffected, in spite of the sizable tax revenues collected. In some plausible situations, such taxes can increase efficiency. The explanation for these surprising results is that the government, by taxing capital income, absorbs a certain fraction of both the expected return and the uncertainty in return. While investors as a result receive a lower expected return, they also bear less risk when they invest, and these two effects are largely offsetting."

Yet, a more recent study by Gentry and Hubbard (2000: 283) asserts:

> "While progressive taxation could in principle encourage entry via insurance for risk-averse entrepreneurs through the tax system or through offering greater incentive to avoid taxes on self-employment income, we find no evidence to support such channels. Our empirical results imply a significant increase in entrepreneurial entry when tax rates are less progressive."

Lastly, Keuschnigg and Nielsen (2004) model the effect a capital gains tax has on both the entrepreneur's effort and the venture capitalist's provision of advice and conclude that even the introduction of a small such tax leads to a first-order welfare loss. So far, to my knowledge they are the only authors who have highlighted how capital gains taxes can influence venture capitalists, making their contribution especially interesting.

Yet, with theoretical arguments pointing both ways, the question of how taxation affects the venture capital market via the demand side, i.e., via its effect on entrepreneurial activity, is ultimately an empirical one. Once again, the studies by Gompers and Lerner (1998c) and Poterba (1989) help shed some light on this issue. Poterba (1989: i) states:

> "Individual capital gains taxes may [...] have a significant influence on the demand for venture funds. These taxes have an important impact on the incentives of entrepreneurs and other employees of start-up firms who forego wage and salary income and accept compensation through corporate stock and options."

The paper does not furnish conclusive empirical evidence on this effect, though. Yet, as we have already seen above, Gompers and Lerner (1998c: 166-167) come to the rescue:

> "Increases in the capital gains tax rates consistently depress contributions to the venture industry, although the effect is only significant for contributions to the entire industry and contributions by pension funds. [...] As Poterba suggests, the effect of

changes in the capital gains tax rate is likely to come through changes in the demand for venture capital. More and better-quality managers become entrepreneurs when the capital gains tax rate declines and the demand for venture capital increases. This increase in demand leads to a greater quantity of venture capital being supplied in equilibrium."

By contrast, Rosen (2005) presents the results of innovative research on the influence of personal income taxes on an entrepreneur's behavior. He finds that, "[a]s tax rates go up, entrepreneurial enterprises grow at a slower rate, they buy less capital, and they are less likely to hire workers."[15]

Regulation of entry

In a widely debated paper, Djankov et al. (2002) have tried to tack exact numbers onto the costs associated with starting a business in a panel of 85 countries. They find that in the U.S. a potential entrepreneur is faced with four procedures and a total cost of 0.0169 times the U.S.' 1999 per capita GDP, including opportunity costs arising from time spent waiting etc., when she wants to start her own business. In Germany, on the other hand, ten procedures await the eager new businessperson, and the total cost of starting a business is roughly twenty times as high as in the U.S., namely 0.3249 times German 1999 per capita GDP.[16]

If we take this one example as indicative of the overall burden that government regulations place on small firms, then it is little wonder that Germany is not just usually perceived as less entrepreneurial than the U.S., but that this notion is indeed based on facts, which would of course mean that there will be less demand for venture capital in Germany than in the U.S.

[15]Rosen (2005: 274)

[16]Djankov et al. (2002: 18-19, table III)

7.3 Views on public policy for venture capital

There is an old joke claiming that when you ask three randomly chosen economists about their view on an economic phenomenon, you will end up with at least four different answers. Yet, if you asked them about the effects of current public policy for venture capital on the economy at large, you might witness a rare near-universal agreement on one thing: There are very few positive effects public policy for venture capital has had so far, if any.[17]

Not all practitioners in Germany share this view, however. A BVK (2004b) study reveals that German private equity firms overwhelmingly endorse the government's involvement in the market. Out of 96 respondents, 50 stated that current public policies adequately address the needs of the market, while 41 said that there was still room for improvement in selected market segments. A more active government role in the early stage realm was suggested most often.[18] How much weight should be attributed to these views remains unclear, however. After all, the subsidized funds that are made available by the German government and the European Union could simply benefit a private equity firms general partners, while leaving the portfolio companies no better off than before. Thus, only if one could show that government funds do not simply crowd out private capital and that government re-financing options indeed benefit (potential) portfolio firms, a convincing case for the notion that (more) financing activity took place only because of the existence of public policies could be made.

[17]Still, a few "dissenters" do exist. See for instance Leleux and Surlemont's (2003: 81) cross-country study of European venture capital markets, which finds that "public involvement seems to cause greater amounts of money to be invested in the industry as a whole." Altogether, their econometric analysis is unconvincing, though, as they base their analysis on private equity, not venture capital, data. In addition, the coefficients they find are quantitatively small, even though they achieve statistical significance. Moreover, they fail to show that not just the venture capital industry, but the economy as a whole benefits from such additional investment.

[18]BVK (2004b: 9)

As has been argued in chapter 2, though, in theory government schemes can considerably strengthen a country's economy. Well-designed public policy schemes that target the venture capital sector can potentially exert a sizable positive effect on the economy.[19] Yet, for all we know, in practice they rarely do. So far, I have argued that the lack of success programs in Germany have met with stems from the fact that most schemes explicitly aim at increasing the supply of venture capital, while indeed only demand is lacking. To further reinforce this notion, the remainder of this chapter is dedicated to a review of a series of articles on public policy for venture capital, most of which have been published in the last few years.

All eyes on demand

Perhaps the strongest endorsement of the demand-side argument can be found in Harding (2002: 59), who "provides evidence to demonstrate [...] that policy has been most effective in countries which have approached the development of a venture capital market through demand rather than supply side measures." One observation stands out in particular:

> "What is interesting [...] is that in all the countries studied apart from America, demand for venture capital has had to be created through policy. Even in countries where entrepreneurship and risk taking was encouraged, such as France, Germany, the UK and the Republic of Ireland, this risk taking was supported by central government grants rather than by private sector finance."

In line with this reasoning is Lawton's (2002: 7) argument that "the challenge for policy is to use venture capital as a tool for creating [small and medium-sized enterprise] growth – rather than growing the venture capital industry in and of itself." McGlue (2002: 56) similarly states: "Venture capital cannot succeed in promoting growth companies unless potential companies are there to be promoted. They will not do so without skilled people

[19] See Lerner (2002) for an excellent summary.

with ideas and a framework (administrative, legal and fiscal) that encourages them to exploit their ideas commercially."[20]

Remarkably, the UK's Small Business Service, a governmental organization comparable to the U.S.' SBA, has set out to promote "investment readiness" among small and medium-sized firms.[21] The idea behind this new initiative is to prop up high-growth companies via consulting and advising until they are "ready" to accept outside equity finance. Interestingly, the necessary consulting services are not provided by the government agency itself, but rather by private-sector firms. Mason and Harrison (2001: 667) quickly reacted to this shift in governmental priorities and published an article with a series of suggested improvements to the program; still, all in all they strongly support the new approach:

> "As the early stage venture capital market has developed in the UK, [...] it has become increasingly clear that there is no effective shortage of capital for investment. [...] It is now clear that the major problem is not the supply of early stage equity finance, nor is it simply an information and connection problem; business angels in particular report that they have considerable funds available for investment and see an increasing number of business plans.
>
> However, they also report a reduction in the quality of the investment opportunities coming forward, which prevents them from investing as frequently as they would like. Against this background, the shift in official policy towards demand-side initiatives, as represented by the HM Treasury/Small Business Service consultation paper on investment readiness, is welcome."

[20] Keuschnigg and Nielsen (2001) discuss optimal public policy more theoretically.
[21] H M Treasury (2001)

European policies

In the discussion so far, German venture capital policy has only been discussed in terms of domestic initiatives. Yet, there is also a European dimension, which mainly manifests itself in various programs the European Union has set up.[22] As Aernoudt (1999: 50) notes, "[r]ecently, on various occasions, European policy makers have stressed the importance of venture capital as one of the main tools for economic growth and job creation. This evolution in political and economic thinking has been translated into a number of concrete actions in the field of venture capital." By now, it probably does not come as a surprise any more that in order to boost venture capital activity, "the European Union, until now relatively absent from the venture capital market, has launched new programmes focusing on direct financing of the setting up and development of venture capital funds (by capital participation or contribution to overheads) as well as on stimulating the general conditions for better access to finance."[23]

As I have argued time and again in this book, though, jumping to the conclusion that supply should be targeted, as the European Union clearly does, is of course not automatically justified. Accordingly, Bottazzi and Da Rin (2002: 232) stress this fact when they assert that "it is far from evident which policy measures would be most appropriate to nurture European venture capital. Here the lack of rigorous investigation is felt most." Their own contribution consists in assembling and analyzing data on more than 500 companies that went public on the pan-European stock exchange *Euro.nm* between its inception in 1997 and its dissolution in 2000. Based on the results from this innovative study, they "argue that venture-backed companies in our sample – i.e. those listed on Euro.nm – do *not* grow and create jobs faster than non venture-backed companies. [...] We also have good news. We find that venture capital does help European innovative companies by

[22]For a broader overview of European technology policy, see Eaton et al. (1998).
[23]Aernoudt (1999: 47)

providing them with financing crucial for their creation and development."[24] In terms of policy implications, they stress that not only sheer quantity, but also the quality of European venture capital should be of central concern to policy makers.[25] Most importantly, "[t]he limitations of our data make us stop short of a final answer, but they resonate well with an increasing body of evidence that European venture capital lacks more human than financial resources."[26]

Not too surprisingly, the German practitioners' view once more deviates from this position. As the BVK (2004b: 9) reports, out of 92 respondents to a survey on fundraising determinants, 16 stated the €500 million ERP/EIF fund set up by the German government in collaboration with the European Investment Fund (EIF) in early 2004 will enhance the prospects for venture capital-fundraising overall, while 61 expect an improvement only for selected funds. Notably, 15 survey respondents assign no importance to this new initiative when it comes to fundraising in the venture capital realm.

What explains the difference between the practitioners' views and the ones held by the majority of academic observers is in all likelihood the fact that practitioners are rational actors and thus welcome subsidies, just like most other businesspersons would, too. After all, the funds made available via government-sponsored supply-side programs often come in the form of low-interest loans and moreover regularly include provisions stating that they only have to be repaid when an investment was successful. In other words, there is near-free money to be had here. Unfortunately, whether schemes such as the new ERP/EIF fund will actually lead to the expected crowding-in of private investment instead of an at least as likely crowding-out thus once more remains an open question.

[24] Bottazzi and Da Rin (2002: 232, emphasis added)
[25] Bottazzi and Da Rin (2002: 233)
[26] Bottazzi and Da Rin (2002: 263)

7.4 Implications

The last question that effectively remains is what can be done about the lack of demand for venture capital. While no clear-cut answers emerge right away, several aspects of the demand-side equation that are relatively easily amenable to public policy intervention stand out.[27] One of them is a call for intensified and improved technology transfer programs, often, but not exclusively, with an eye towards commercialization of intellectual property that was created in academic settings.[28] Here the U.S. seems to have an especially pronounced edge over most, if not all, other countries in the world, yet in principle playing catch-up should be feasible at least to a certain extent.[29] Also, as Romer (2000) has argued, inducing more students to choose careers in engineering and science might yield considerable benefits in the long run, too, even irrespective of such students' later decision to request venture capital funding for a project.

Finally, a look to Silicon Valley confirms the notion that many of the brightest people working in the most successful high-tech companies do not have U.S. passports. Put differently, concerted efforts by European governments to attract highly skilled immigrants represent another plausible venue for strengthening the venture capital industry and the overall economy in Europe. Finally, Harding (2002: 75) raises some additional points which are easily overlooked:

> "Perhaps the most effective measures, however, are those which actually cost very little. Publicity and promotion of success stories have paid dividends across Europe, in Singapore and in the U.S. It is these measures which create changes in the nature of demand for venture capital – people hear stories about individual entrepreneurs who have used this type of finance and learn

[27] See Keuschnigg and Nielsen (2005) for a closely related discussion and a series of further ideas.

[28] Bozeman (2000) provides a comprehensive introduction to such programs.

[29] See Goldfarb and Henrekson (2003) for a comparative analysis of the U.S. and Sweden in this area.

> about how to access it accordingly. It is this type of transparency which is lacking in the UK in particular. Yet transparency leads to better information, and better information gives the market the best possible boost."

Still, it should be clear that none of these proposals constitute a quick fix. More likely, the venture capital sector in Germany will in all likelihood mature slowly, but could eventually reach the same level of activity as the U.S.[30] Ultimately, the extent to which Germany will be able to catch up with the U.S. will be determined by the demand for venture capital, an area in which the American economy is still far ahead of all European economies.[31]

[30] The "same" level would of course be a relative one, for instance one expressed as a fraction of GDP.

[31] This relates to a recent argument by Gompers et al. (2003), who posit that a successful venture capital scene might feed on itself, as more and more potential entrepreneurs have come into contact with venture capitalists the larger the sector, and will therefore be more likely to request such services once they start their own businesses.

Chapter 8

Nothing ventured?

> We have not succeeded in answering all our problems. The answers we have found only serve to raise a whole set of new questions. In some ways we feel we are as confused as ever, but we believe we are confused on a higher level and about more important things.
>
> (B. Øksendal, 1985)

This book set out to describe and evaluate public policy for venture capital in the U.S. and Germany. While it certainly has not answered all questions along the way, at least one insight should by now be firmly ingrained in the minds of this discussion's readers. Not supply of, but demand for venture capital is the crucial ingredient that American and German policy makers have to add to their equations if they want to see their domestic venture capital markets flourish and thereby ultimately have the two countries' economies themselves prosper.

While in the U.S. a good case for active government policy in the venture capital realm is hard to discern as the industry has apparently reached a self-sustaining size, a good case can be made for such activity in Germany both on a theoretical level and based on the empirical data presented in this book, which makes clear that there is still a lot of room for improvement. However, the current governmental practice of targeting the supply of venture capital appears heavily misguided and should be abandoned in favor of efforts to promote more demand for venture capital.

As the quote above alludes to, many questions still remain unanswered. First and foremost, solid econometric evidence at the program, industry, and firm-level is sorely missing in the literature on the German venture capital market. Beyond some more or less impressionistic descriptions of the major public policy initiatives, not much attention has been paid to a thorough analysis of these schemes. Equally troubling is the state of knowledge about the German venture capital market as a whole. As chapter 4 made clear, even the more recent data provided by the BVK is so far often spotty, inconsistent, and certainly not as comprehensive as one would wish for. It is thus not only the case that the German venture capital market itself is trailing its U.S. counterpart by a considerable margin, but that the same is also still true for our knowledge about it.

Data appendix

VC and PE data: Data on venture capital activity is based on own computations using the BVK Statistik (various years; 1991-2004) for Germany and the NVCA Yearbook (2004) for the U.S., which includes updated information for the years 1981 to 2003. 2004 data for the U.S. is taken from the April 18, 2005, NVCA press release "Venture capital and private equity fundraising maintains solid pace in Q1 2005." (available at www.nvca.org)

GDP data: German GDP data is from Statistisches Bundesamt, Fachserie 18, Reihe S. 21 ("Revidierte Ergebnisse 1970 bis 2004"), Tabelle 1.1.1; version of 13 July 2005 (http://www.destatis.de/download/veroe/lreihenab1970.xls). US GDP data is taken from the Bureau of Economic Analysis' website (available at http://www.bea.doc.gov/bea/dn/gdplev.xls); version of 28 June 2005.

PEMC data: Public equity market capitalization data for Germany, which is only available from 1999 on, is taken from the Deutsche Bundesbank's Kapitalmarktstatistik / Zeitreihe WU080U; it includes "alle Gesellschaften, deren Aktien zum Amtlichen Markt oder zum Geregelten Markt zugelassen sind; ferner auch Gesellschaften, deren Aktien im Freiverkehr gehandelt werden." Version of 12 July 2005. US public equity data is based upon the Federal Reserve's "Flow of Funds Accounts of the United States" (1985-1994 and 1995-2004), table L.213 ("Corporate Equities"), line 21 ("Market value of domestic corporations"); version of 09 June 2005.

Ia. German private equity and venture capital overview data, 1991-2004 (Part I, 1991-1997)

Year	1991	1992	1993	1994	1995	1996	1997
	BVK only	Gesamtmarkt	Gesamtmarkt	Gesamtmarkt	Gesamtmarkt	Gesamtmarkt	Gesamtmarkt
New funds raised	818.41	862.75	205.73	291.81	201.08	332.16	2586.91
Capital under management	2838.17	4016.44	4222.18	4513.99	4715.07	5047.22	7634.13
Disbursements	508.99	628.46	568.53	740.59	583.55	698.73	1332.71
Total funds invested	1983.06	2623.40	2747.95	3157.94	3203.62	3390.72	3961.52
Exits	na	128.65	205.90	271.05	303.79	271.01	515.64
new "real VC" invested	369.43	324.11	399.19	580.13	389.42	433.39	826.60
"real VC" among funds invested	1415.96	1856.81	1992.06	2149.30	2276.86	2347.65	2689.71
"real VC" as % of disbursements	0.7258	0.5157	0.7021	0.7833	0.6673	0.6203	0.6202
"real VC" as % of funds invested	0.7140	0.7078	0.7249	0.6806	0.7107	0.6924	0.6790
German GDP in current prices	1502200.00	1613200.00	1654200.00	1735500.00	1801300.00	1833700.00	1871600.00
New PE raised as % of GDP	0.054481	0.053481	0.012437	0.016814	0.011163	0.018114	0.138219
Capital under management as % of GDP	0.188934	0.248974	0.255240	0.260097	0.261759	0.275248	0.407893
Disbursements as % of GDP	0.033883	0.038958	0.034369	0.042673	0.032396	0.038105	0.071207
Total funds invested as % of GDP	0.132010	0.162621	0.166120	0.181961	0.177850	0.184911	0.211665
Exits as % of GDP	na	0.007975	0.012447	0.015618	0.016865	0.014779	0.027551
"real VC" disbursed as % of GDP	0.024593	0.020091	0.024132	0.033427	0.021619	0.023635	0.044165
"real VC" invested as % of GDP	0.094259	0.115101	0.120425	0.123843	0.126401	0.128028	0.143712
Public equity market cap	na	na	na	na	na	na	na
New PE raised as % of public market cap	na	na	na	na	na	na	na
Capital under mgt. as % of public market cap	na	na	na	na	na	na	na
Disbursements as % of public market cap	na	na	na	na	na	na	na
Total funds invested as % of public market cap	na	na	na	na	na	na	na
Exits as % of public market cap	na	na	na	na	na	na	na
"real VC" disbursed as % of public market cap	na	na	na	na	na	na	na
"real VC" invested as % of public market cap	na	na	na	na	na	na	na

All figures are in million euros, unless otherwise noted. "real VC" = seed + start-up + expansion

Sources: see the description on page 115

Ib. German private equity and venture capital overview data, 1991-2004 (Part II, 1998-2004)

Year	1998	1999	2000	2001	2002	2003	2004
	Gesamtmarkt	Gesamtmarkt	Gesamtmarkt	BVK only	BVK only	BVK only	BVK only
New funds raised	1887.74	4630.06	6113.85	10319.39	3669.53	6350.02	1983.13
Capital under management	9521.87	13640.51	20126.98	28492.16	33252.46	na	na
Disbursements	1961.71	3158.82	4766.60	4434.89	2506.19	2415.40	3765.79
Total funds invested	5388.47	7896.47	11478.76	15844.00	16655.13	17887.62	20256.00
Exits	384.56	834.23	1307.10	1855.23	2131.84	820.46	1481.40
new "real VC" invested	1054.89	2134.15	3328.77	2530.58	1265.33	666.20	965.38
"real VC" among funds invested	3313.94	5113.40	7644.66	na	na	na	na
"real VC" as % of disbursements	0.5377	0.6756	0.6984	0.5706	0.5049	0.2758	0.2564
"real VC" as % of funds invested	0.6150	0.6476	0.6660	na	na	na	na
German GDP in current prices	1929400.00	1978600.00	2030000.00	2074000.00	2107300.00	2128200.00	2177000.00
New PE raised as % of GDP	0.097841	0.234007	0.301175	0.497560	0.174134	0.298375	0.091095
Capital under management as % of GDP	0.493514	0.689402	0.991477	1.373778	1.577965	na	na
Disbursements as % of GDP	0.101675	0.159649	0.234808	0.213833	0.118929	0.113495	0.172981
Total funds invested as % of GDP	0.279282	0.399094	0.565456	0.763934	0.790354	0.840505	0.930455
Exits as % of GDP	0.019932	0.042163	0.064389	0.089452	0.101165	0.038552	0.068048
"real VC" disbursed as % of GDP	0.054675	0.107862	0.163979	0.122014	0.060045	0.031303	0.044345
"real VC" invested as % of GDP	0.171760	0.258435	0.376584	na	na	na	na
Public equity market cap		1603304.00	1353000.00	1205613.00	647498.00	851001.00	887217.00
New PE raised as % of public market cap	na	0.288783	0.451874	0.855945	0.566725	0.746182	0.223523
Capital under mgt. as % of public market cap	na	0.850775	1.487582	2.363292	5.135531	na	na
Disbursements as % of public market cap	na	0.197019	0.352298	0.367854	0.387058	0.283830	0.424450
Total funds invested as % of public market cap	na	0.492512	0.848393	1.314186	2.572229	2.101951	2.283094
Exits as % of public market cap	na	0.052032	0.096608	0.153883	0.329243	0.096411	0.166972
"real VC" disbursed as % of public market cap	na	0.133109	0.246029	0.209900	0.195418	0.078284	0.108810
"real VC" invested as % of public market cap	na	0.318929	0.565015	na	na	na	na

All figures are in million euros, unless otherwise noted. "real VC" = seed + start-up + expansion

Sources: see the description on page 115

IIa. Comparison of US and German venture capital data, weighed by GDP & public equity market capitalization (PEMC), 1991-2004 (Part I, 1991-1997)

Year	1991	1992	1993	1994	1995	1996	1997
new VC raised (BVK) in Germany as fraction of GDP	na	na	na	na	na	na	na
new VC raised in the US as fraction of GDP	0.000345	0.000826	0.000595	0.001104	0.001353	0.001485	0.002196
VC disbursed in Germany as fraction of GDP	0.000246	0.000201	0.000241	0.000334	0.000216	0.000236	0.000442
VC disbursed in the US as fraction of GDP	0.000374	0.000559	0.000550	0.000586	0.001032	0.001474	0.001780
new VC raised (BVK) in Germany as PEMC fraction	na	na	na	na	na	na	na
new VC raised in the US as fraction of PEMC	0.000467	0.001054	0.000708	0.001413	0.001339	0.001286	0.001547
VC disbursed in Germany as fraction of PEMC	na	na	na	na	na	na	na
VC disbursed in the US as fraction of PEMC	0.000506	0.000713	0.000654	0.000751	0.001022	0.001276	0.001254
VC disbursed as a fraction of VC raised in Germany	na	na	na	na	na	na	na
VC disbursed as a fraction of VC raised in the US	1.083977	0.676459	0.923611	0.531245	0.763116	0.992344	0.810518
German GDP in current prices in EUR mio.	1502200.00	1613200	1654200	1735500	1801300	1833700	1871600
new VC raised in Germany in EUR mio. (BVK only)	na	na	na	na	na	na	na
VC disbursed in Germany in EUR mio.	369.43	324.11	399.19	580.13	389.42	433.39	826.60
German public equity market cap in EUR mio.	na	na	na	na	na	na	na
US GDP in current prices in USD mio.	5995900	6337700	6657400	7072200	7397700	7816900	8304300
new VC raised in the US in USD mio.	2070.80	5235.50	3961.30	7806.00	10009.10	11611.10	18235.00
VC disbursed in the US in USD mio.	2244.70	3541.60	3658.70	4146.90	7638.10	11522.20	14779.80
VC under management in USD mio.	29022.20	29361.90	30636.00	35298.80	40400.00	48159.60	63154.10
US public equity market cap in USD mio.	4434900	4968400	5594100	5523300	7474400	9030800	11788100

Sources: see the description on page 115

IIb. Comparison of US and German venture capital data, weighed by GDP & public equity market capitalization (PEMC), 1991-2004 (Part II, 1998-2004)

Year	1998	1999	2000	2001	2002	2003	2004
new VC raised (BVK) in Germany as fraction of GDP	na	0.000975	0.002180	0.002075	0.000480	0.000289	0.000280
new VC raised in the US as fraction of GDP	0.003478	0.006277	0.010739	0.003687	0.000863	0.000996	na
VC disbursed in Germany as fraction of GDP	0.000547	0.001079	0.001640	0.001220	0.000600	0.000313	0.000443
VC disbursed in the US as fraction of GDP	0.002429	0.005874	0.010783	0.004007	0.002043	0.001643	na
new VC raised (BVK) in Germany as PEMC fraction	na	0.001204	0.003271	0.003570	0.001564	0.000722	0.000688
new VC raised in the US as fraction of PEMC	0.002213	0.003391	0.006851	0.002804	0.000891	0.000840	na
VC disbursed in Germany as fraction of PEMC	na	0.001331	0.002460	0.002099	0.001954	0.000783	0.001088
VC disbursed in the US as fraction of PEMC	0.001545	0.003173	0.006879	0.003048	0.002108	0.001386	na
VC disbursed as a fraction of VC raised in Germany	na	1.105914	0.752244	0.587918	1.249807	1.084151	1.581398
VC disbursed as a fraction of VC raised in the US	0.698301	0.935745	1.004027	1.086826	2.365834	1.649889	na
German GDP in current prices in EUR mio.	1929400	1978600	2030000	2074000	2107300	2128200	2177000
new VC raised in Germany in EUR mio. (BVK only)	na	1929.76	4425.12	4304.31	1012.42	614.49	610.46
VC disbursed in Germany in EUR mio.	1054.89	2134.15	3328.77	2530.58	1265.33	666.20	965.38
German public equity market cap in EUR mio.	na	1603304	1353000	1205613	647498	851001	887217
US GDP in current prices in USD mio.	8747000	9268400	9817000	10128000	10487000	11004000	11735000
new VC raised in the US in USD mio.	30423.00	58178.00	105428.60	37338.90	9054.10	10955.10	na
VC disbursed in the US in USD mio.	21244.40	54439.80	105853.20	40580.90	21420.50	18074.70	na
VC under management in USD mio.	90825.10	148903.90	228235.80	256890.30	258479.00	257529.10	na
US public equity market cap in USD mio.	13747800	17158000	15388600	13316100	10163300	13042100	14197600

Sources: see the description on page 115

Bibliography

Abbott, Charles C. and Eugene M. Zuckert. 1941. "Venture Capital and Taxation." *Quarterly Journal of Economics* 55(4): 667-682.

Aernoudt, Rudy. 1999. "European policy towards venture capital: myth or reality?" *Venture Capital* 1(1): 47-58.

Aghion, Philippe and Peter Howitt. 1998. *Endogenous Growth Theory.* Cambridge, MA: MIT Press.

Albach, Horst and Dieter Köster. 1997. "Risikokapital in Deutschland." Discussion Paper FS IV 97 – 17. Wissenschaftszentrum Berlin für Sozialforschung.

Anand, Bharat N. and Alexander Galetovic. 2000a. "Information, Nonexcludability, and Financial Market Structure." *Journal of Business* 73(3): 357-402.

Anand, Bharat N. and Alexander Galetovic. 2000b. "Weak Property Rights and Holdup in R&D." *Journal of Economics & Management Strategy* 9(4): 615-642.

Audretsch, David B., Albert N. Link, and John T. Scott. 2002. "Public/ private technology partnerships: evaluating SBIR-supported research." *Research Policy* 31: 145-158.

Baldwin, William L. and John T. Scott. 1987. *Market Structure and Technological Change.* New York: Harwood Publishers.

Barkley, David L., Deborah M. Markley, and Julia Sass Rubin. 2001. "Certified Capital Companies (CAPCOs): Strengths and Shortcomings of the Latest Wave in State-Assisted Venture Capital Programs." *Economic Development Quarterly* 15(4): 350-366.

Bartlett, Joseph W. 1995. *Equity Finance: Venture Capital, Buyouts, Restructurings and Reorganizations.* New York: Wiley.

Bartlett, Joseph W. 1999. *Fundamentals of Venture Capital.* Lanham: Madison Books.

Baum, Joel A.C. and Brian S. Silverman. 2004. "Picking winners or building them? Alliance, intellectual, and human capital as selection criteria in venture financing and performance of biotechnology startups." *Journal of Business Venturing* 19: 411-436.

Becker, Ralf and Thomas Hellmann. 2005. "The Genesis of Venture Capital: Lessons from the German Experience." in: Kanniainen, Vesa and Christian Keuschnigg. eds. *Venture Capital, Entrepreneurship, and Public Policy.* CESifo Seminar Series. Cambridge, MA: MIT Press, pp. 33-67.

Belke, Ansgar, Rainer Fehn, and Neil Foster. 2005. "Venture Capital Investment and Labor Market Performance: A Panel Data Analysis." in: Kanniainen, Vesa and Christian Keuschnigg. eds. *Venture Capital, Entrepreneurship, and Public Policy.* CESifo Seminar Series. Cambridge, MA: MIT Press, pp. 97-126.

Belsley, David A., Edwin Kuh, and Roy E. Welsch. 1980. *Regression Diagnostics. Identifying Influential Data and Sources of Collinearity.* New York, NY: Wiley Interscience.

Benjamin, Gerald A. and Ellen J. Sandles. 1998. "Angel Investors: Culling the Waters for Private Equity." *Journal of Private Equity* 1(3): 41-59.

Bergemann, Dirk and Ulrich Hege. 1998. "Venture capital financing, moral hazard, and learning." *Journal of Banking & Finance* 22: 703-735.

Black, Bernard S. and Ronald J. Gilson. 1998. "Venture capital and the structure of capital markets: banks versus stock markets." *Journal of Financial Economics* 47: 243-277.

Boadway, Robin and Jean-François Tremblay. 2005. "Public Economics and Start-up Entrepreneurs." in: Kanniainen, Vesa and Christian Keuschnigg. eds. *Venture Capital, Entrepreneurship, and Public Policy.* CESifo Seminar Series. Cambridge, MA: MIT Press, pp. 181-219.

Bottazzi, Laura and Marco Da Rin. 2002. "Venture capital in Europe and the financing of innovative companies." *Economic Policy*, April: 231-269.

Bozeman, Barry. 2000. "Technology transfer and public policy: a review of research and theory." *Research Policy* 29: 627-655.

Brettel, Malte. 2002. "German Business Angels in International Comparison." *Journal of Private Equity* 5(2): 53-67.

Bruhns, Klaus. 1992. *Die Förderung von Kapitalbeteiligungsgesellschaften als Instrument der Mittelstandspolitik. Eine kritische Analyse der Wirkungen und Einsatzmöglichkeiten.* Pfaffenweiler: Centaurus-Verlagsgesellschaft.

Brunswig, Rolf. 1984. "Der S-Siegerlandfonds." *Zeitschrift für das gesamte Kreditwesen* 4: 138-143.

Büschgen, Hans E. 1985a. "Venture Capital – der deutsche Ansatz." *Die Bank* 5/85: 220-226.

Büschgen, Hans E. 1985b. "Banken und Venture-Capital-Finanzierung." *Die Bank* 6/85: 284-292.

Bulow, Jeremy I. and Lawrence H. Summers. 1984. "The Taxation of Risky Assets." *Journal of Political Economy* 92(1): 20-39.

BVK. 2004 and earlier (yearly). *BVK Statistik.* Berlin: Bundesverband Deutscher Kapitalbeteiligungsgesellschaften e.V.

BVK. 2004b. "Fundraising 2004 – Einschätzung der aktuellen Fundraising-Situation deutscher Private Equity-Gesellschaften." *BVK Studie*, September 29, Berlin: Bundesverband Deutscher Kapitalbeteiligungsgesellschaften e.V.

BVK. 2005. "IPO-Markt 2005 – Einschätzung der aktuellen Börsensituation aus Sicht der deutschen Beteiligungsgesellschaften." *BVK Studie*, July 20, 2005, Berlin: Bundesverband Deutscher Kapitalbeteiligungsgesellschaften e.V.

Bygrave, William D. and Jeffry A. Timmons. 1992. *Venture Capital at the Crossroads.* Boston: HBS Press.

Cadenhead, Gary M., Jürgen Weber, Malte Brettel, Cyril Jaugey, and Cornelius Rost. 2000. "Business Angels in Germany: How Business Angels in Germany Help New Entrepreneurs." *Journal of Private Equity* 4(1): 50-58.

Callison, J. William. 2000. "Venture Capital and Corporate Governance: Evolving the Limited Liability Company to Finance the Entrepreneurial Business." *The Journal of Corporation Law*, Fall: 97-124.

Chang, Connie K. N., Stephanie S. Shipp, and Andrew J. Wang. 2002. "The Advanced Technology Program: a public-private partnership for early stage technology development." *Venture Capital* 4(4): 363-370.

Chesbrough, Henry W. 2002. "Making Sense of Corporate Venture Capital." *Harvard Business Review*, March: 4-11.

Cochrane, John H. 2005. "The risk and return of venture capital." *Journal of Financial Economics* 75: 3-52.

Cornelius, Barbara. 2005. "The institutionalisation of venture capital." *Technovation* 25: 599-608.

Cumming, Douglas J. 2005. "Agency costs, institutions, learning, and taxation in venture capital contracting." *Journal of Business Venturing* 20: 573-622.

Cumming, Douglas, Grant Fleming, and Jo-Ann Suchard. 2005 "Venture capitalist value-added activities, fundraising and drawdowns." *Journal of Banking & Finance* 29: 295-331.

David, Paul A., Bronwyn H. Hall, and Andrew A. Toole. 2000. "Is public R&D a complement or substitute for private R&D? A review of the econometric evidence." *Research Policy* 29: 497-529.

Davila, Antonio, George Foster, and Mahendra Gupta. 2003. "Venture capital financing and the growth of startup firms." *Journal of Business Venturing* 18: 689-708.

Deutsche Bundesbank. 2000. "The market for venture capital in Germany." *Deutsche Bundesbank Monthly Report*, October: 15-29.

Dietz, Martin D. 2002. "Risk, Self Selection, and Advice: Banks versus Venture Capitalists." Working paper, Universität St. Gallen (IFF-HSG), January 10.

Djankov, Simeon, Rafael La Porta, Florencio Lopez-de-Silanes, and Andrei Shleifer. 2002. "The regulation of entry." *Quarterly Journal of Economics* 117(1): 1-37.

Eaton, Jonathan, Eva Gutierrez, and Samuel Kortum. 1998. "European technology policy." *Economic Policy*, October: 405-438.

EVCA. 1987. *EVCA Yearbook. Venture Capital in Europe 1987.* Report prepared by KPMG Peat Marwick McLintock, London.

Fenn, George W., Nellie Liang, and Stephen Prowse. 1995. *The Economics of the Private Equity Market.* Washington, D.C.: Board of Governors of the Federal Reserve System.

Fiedler, Marc-Oliver and Thomas Hellmann. 2001. "Against all odds: The Late but Rapid Development of the German Venture Capital Industry." *Journal of Private Equity* 4(4): 31-45.

Field, Alexander J. 2003. "The Most Technologically Progressive Decade of the Century." *American Economic Review* 93(4): 1399-1413.

Florida, Richard. 1994. "What Start-ups Don't Need is Money." *Inc.*, April: 27-28.

Florin, Juan. 2005. "Is venture capital worth it? Effects of firm performance and founder returns." *Journal of Business Venturing* 20: 113-135.

Francis, Bill, Iftekhar Hasan, and Feng Li. 2001. "Underpricing of Foreign and Domestic IPOs in the U.S. Market: Empirical Evidence." *Financial Markets, Institutions & Instruments* 10(1): 1-18.

Franzke, Stefanie, Stefanie Grohs, and Christian Laux. 2003. "Initial Public Offerings and Venture Capital in Germany." *CFS Working Paper No. 2003/26*, University Frankfurt/Main, April.

Frommann, Holger. 1992. "Venture Capital in Deutschland - Rückblick auf ein Vierteljahrhundert." in: Bundesverband deutscher Kapitalbeteiligungsgesellschaften. *BVK Jahrbuch 1992.* Berlin: BVK, pp. 101-106.

Frommann, Holger. 1993. "Entwicklungstrends am deutschen Beteiligungsmarkt." in: Bundesverband deutscher Kapitalbeteiligungsgesellschaften. *BVK Jahrbuch 1993.* Berlin: BVK, pp. 11-31.

Frommann, Holger and Attila Dahmann. 2003. *Zur volkswirtschaftlichen Bedeutung von Private Equity und Venture Capital.* Berlin: BVK.

Gaida, Michael. 2002. *Venture Capital in Deutschland und den USA. Finanzierung von Start-ups im Gefüge von Staat, Banken und Börsen.* Wiesbaden: Deutscher Universitäts-Verlag.

Gans, Joshua, David H. Hsu, and Scott Stern. 2002. "When does start-up innovation spur the gale of creative destruction?" *RAND Journal of Economics* 33(4): 571-586.

Gentry, William M. and R. Glenn Hubbard. 2000. "Tax Policy and Entrepreneurial Entry." *American Economic Review* 90(2): 283-287.

Gerke, Wolfgang. 1975. "Was kann die Wagnisfinanzierungs-GmbH (WFG) leisten?" *Zeitschrift für das gesamte Kreditwesen* 16: 761-764.

Gilson, Ronald J. 2002. "Engineering a Venture Capital Market: Lessons from the American Experience." John M. Olin Program in Law and Economics Working Paper 248, Stanford Law School, November.

Gilson, Ronald J. and David M. Schizer. 2003. "Understanding venture capital structure: A tax explanation for convertible preferred stock." *Harvard Law Review* 116(3): 874-916.

Giudici, Giancarlo and Stefano Paleari. 2000. "The Optimal Staging of Venture Capital Financing when Entrepreneurs Extract Private Benefits from Their Firms." *Enterprise & Innovation Management Studies* 1(2): 153-174.

Global Insight, Inc. 2004. "Venture Impact 2004: Venture Capital Benefits to the U.S. Economy." Research report, Waltham, MA: Global Insight, Inc. and Arlington, VA: NVCA.

Goldfarb, Brent and Magnus Henrekson. 2003. "Bottom-up versus top-down policies towards the commercialization of university intellectual property." *Research Policy* 32: 639-658.

Gompers, Paul A. 1995. "Optimal Investment, Monitoring, and the Staging of Venture Capital." *Journal of Finance* 50: 1461-1489.

Gompers, Paul A. 1996. "Grandstanding in the venture capital industry." *Journal of Financial Economics* 42: 133-156.

Gompers, Paul A. and Josh Lerner. 1998a. "Conflict of Interest in the Issuance of Public Securities: Evidence from Venture Capital." NBER Working Paper No. 6847, December.

Gompers, Paul A. and Josh Lerner. 1998b. "The Determinants of Corporate Venture Capital Success: Organizational Structure, Incentives, and Complementaries." NBER Working Paper No. 6725, September.

Gompers, Paul A. and Josh Lerner. 1998c. "What Drives Venture Capital Fundraising?" *Brookings Papers on Economic Activity. Microeconomics* Vol. 1998: 149-192.

Gompers, Paul A. and Josh Lerner. 1999. *The Venture Capital Cycle.* Cambridge: MIT Press.

Gompers, Paul A. and Josh Lerner. 2001a. *The Money of Invention.* Boston: HBS Press.

Gompers, Paul A. and Josh Lerner. 2001b. "The Venture Capital Revolution." *Journal of Economic Perspectives* 15(2): 145-168.

Gompers, Paul A., Josh Lerner, and David Scharfstein. 2003. "Entrepreneurial Spawning: Public Corporations and the Genesis of New Ventures, 1986 – 1999." Working paper, HBS.

Gordon, Roger H. 1985. "Taxation of corporate capital income: Tax revenues versus tax distortions." *Quarterly Journal of Economics* 100(1): 1-27.

Gordon, Steven. 1998. "Small Business Investment Companies: A Venture Capital Structure of Choice?" *Journal of Private Equity* 2(1): 45-55.

Gorman, Michael and William A. Sahlman. 1989. "What Do Venture Capitalists Do?" *Journal of Business Venturing* 4: 231-248.

Grisebach, Rolf. 1989. *Innovationsfinanzierung durch Venture Capital. Eine juritische und ökonomische Analyse.* München: VVF.

Güllmann, Peter. 2000. *Die Rolle des Staates bei der Mobilisierung von (privatem) Risikokapital im Seed- und Start-up-Segment: Am Beispiel von Deutschland, Großbritannien und den Niederlanden.* Lohmar: Josef Eul.

Hall, Bronwyn H. 2002. "The Financing of Research and Development." *Oxford Review of Economic Policy* 18(1): 35-51.

Hamilton, James D. 1994. *Time Series Analysis.* Princeton, NJ: Princeton University Press.

Harding, Rebecca. 2002. "Plugging the knowledge gap: an international comparison of the role for policy in the venture capital market." *Venture Capital* 4(1): 59-76.

Harrison, M. Elizabeth. 1990. *The West German Venture Capital Market – An Analysis of its Market Structure and Economic Performance.* Europäische Hochschulschriften: Reihe 5, Bd. 946. Frankfurt am Main: Peter Lang.

Hauser, James L. 2003. "The ERISA implications of pension plan investments in venture capital funds." *Benefits Law Journal* 16(1): 74-85.

Hellmann, Thomas. 1998. "The allocation of control rights in venture capital contracts." *RAND Journal of Economics* 29(1): 57-76.

Hellmann, Thomas. 2000. "IPOs, Acquisitions and the Use of Convertible Securities in Venture Capital." Working paper. Graduate School of Business, Stanford University, December.

Hellmann, Thomas. 2002. "A theory of strategic venture investing." *Journal of Financial Economics* 64: 285-314.

Hellmann, Thomas and Manju Puri. 2000. "The Interaction Between Product Market and Financing Strategy: The Role of Venture Capital." *The Review of Financial Studies* 13(4): 959-984.

Hellmann, Thomas and Manju Puri. 2002. "Venture Capital and the Professionalization of Start-up Firms: Empirical Evidence." *Journal of Finance* 57(1): 169-197.

Henderson, Rebecca. 1993. "Underinvestment and Incompetence as Responses to Radical Innovation: Evidence from the Photolithographic Alignment Equipment Industry." *RAND Journal of Economics* 24(2): 248-270.

H M Treasury. 2001. "'Investment readiness': helping enterprises access equity finance for growth." H M Treasury/Small Business Service consultation document, March 30.

Holmstrom, Bengt. 1989. "Agency Costs and Innovation." *Journal of Economic Behavior and Organization* 12(2): 305-327.

Howitt, Peter. 2000. "Endogenous Growth and Cross-Country Income Differences." *American Economic Review* 90(4): 829-846.

Huang, Haizhou and Chenggang Xu. 2003. "Financial syndication and R&D." *Economics Letters* 80: 141-146.

Hyytinen, Ari. 2005. "How Important Are Exits for Venture Capital Finance? Evidence from Finland." in: Kanniainen, Vesa and Christian Keuschnigg. eds. *Venture Capital, Entrepreneurship, and Public Policy*. CESifo Seminar Series. Cambridge, MA: MIT Press, pp. 127-149.

Industriemagazin. 1985. "Venture Capital: Zuviel Geld." *Industriemagazin*, Oktober 1985: 146-153.

Jeng, Leslie A. and Philippe C. Wells. 2000. "The determinants of venture capital funding: evidence across countries." *Journal of Corporate Finance* 6: 241-289.

Jones, Charles I. 1995. "R & D-Based Models of Economic Growth." *Journal of Political Economy* 103(4): 759-784.

Jones, Charles I. 1999. "Growth: With or Without Scale Effects?" *American Economic Review* 89(2): 139-144.

Jones, Charles I. 2002. *Introduction to Economic Growth.* 2nd ed. New York: Norton.

Jones, Charles I. and John C. Williams. 1998. "Measuring the social return to R&D." *Quarterly Journal of Economics* 113(4): 1119-1135.

Kaplan, Steven N. and Per Strömberg. 2000. "How Do Venture Capitalists Choose and Manage Their Investments?" Working paper, University of Chicago, September.

Kaplan, Steven N. and Per Strömberg. 2001. "Venture Capitalists as Principals: Contracting, Screening, and Monitoring." *AEA Papers and Proceedings* 91(2): 426-430.

Kaplan, Steven N. and Per Strömberg. 2003. "Financial Contracting Theory Meets the Real World: An Empirical Analysis of Venture Capital Contracts." *Review of Economic Studies* 70: 281-315.

Keuschnigg, Christian. 2003. "Optimal public policy for venture capital backed growth." CEPR Discussion Paper No. 3850, March.

Keuschnigg, Christian. 2004. "Venture Capital Backed Growth." *Journal of Economic Growth* 9: 239-261.

Keuschnigg, Christian and Søren Bo Nielsen. 2001. "Public Policy for Venture Capital." *International Tax and Public Finance* 8: 557-572.

Keuschnigg, Christian and Søren Bo Nielsen. 2004. "Start-ups, venture capitalists, and the capital gains tax." *Journal of Public Economics* 88: 1011-1042.

Keuschnigg, Christian and Søren Bo Nielsen. 2005. "Public Policy for Start-up Entrepreneurship with Venture Capital and Bank Finance." in: Kanniainen, Vesa and Christian Keuschnigg. eds. *Venture Capital, Entrepreneurship, and Public Policy.* CESifo Seminar Series. Cambridge, MA: MIT Press, pp. 221-250.

Klette, Tor Jakob, Jarle Møen, and Zvi Griliches. 2000. "Do subsidies to commercial R&D reduce market failures? Microeconometric evaluation studies." *Research Policy* 29: 471-495.

Kortum, Samuel and Josh Lerner. 2001. "Does Venture Capital Spur Innovation?" in: Gary D. Libecap. ed. *Entrepreneurial Inputs and Outcomes: New Studies of Entrepreneurship in the United States (Advances in the Study of Entrepreneurship, Innovation, and Economic Growth, Volume 13).* Amsterdam: JAI Press, pp. 1-44.

Landier, Augustin. 2001. "Start-up Financing: Banks vs. Venture Capital." Working Paper. Department of Economics, MIT, November 19.

Lawton, Thomas C. 2002. "Missing the target: assessing the role of government in bridging the European equity gap and enhancing economic growth." *Venture Capital* 4(1): 7-23.

Lee, Peggy M. and Sunil Wahal. 2004. "Grandstanding, certification and the underpricing of venture capital backed IPOs." *Journal of Financial Economics* 73: 375-407.

Leleux, Benoît and Bernard Surlemont. 2003. "Public versus private venture capital: seeding or crowding out? A pan-European analysis." *Journal of Business Venturing* 18: 81-104.

Leopold, Günther and Holger Frommann. 1998. *Eigenkapital für den Mittelstand. Venture Capital im In- und Ausland.*

Lerner, Josh. 1995. "Venture Capitalists and the Oversight of Private Firms." *Journal of Finance* 50: 301-318.

Lerner, Josh. 1998. "'Angel' financing and public policy: An overview." *Journal of Banking and Finance* 22: 773-783.

Lerner, Josh. 1999. "The Government as Venture Capitalist: The Long-Run Impact of the SBIR Program." *Journal of Business* 72(3): 285-318.

Lerner, Josh. 2000. *Venture Capital and Private Equity: A Casebook.* New York: Wiley.

Lerner, Josh. 2002. "When bureaucrats meet entrepreneurs: The design of effective 'public venture capital' programmes." *Economic Journal* 112 (February): F73-F84.

Lewis, Michael. 2000. *The New New Thing.* New York: Penguin Books.

Link, Albert N., David Paton, and Donald S. Siegel. 2002. "An analysis of policy initiatives to promote strategic research partnerships." *Research Policy* 31: 1459-1466.

Lloyd Fonds AG. 2003. "Newsletter April 2003", accessed online on November 10, 2003, at http://www.lloydfonds.de/_download/newsletter04-2003.pdf

Long, J. Scott and Laurie H. Ervin. 2000. "Using Heteroscedasticity Consistent Standard Errors in the Liner Regression Model." *American Statistician* 54(3): 217-224.

Martin, Stephen and John T. Scott. 2000. "The nature of innovation market failure and the design of public support for private innovation." *Research Policy* 29: 437-447.

Martinelli, César. 1997. "Small firms, borrowing constraints, and reputation." *Journal of Economic Behavior & Organization* 33: 91-105.

Mason, Colin M. and Richard T. Harrison. 1996. "Why 'Business Angels' Say No: A Case Study of Opportunities Rejected by an Informal Investor Syndicate." *International Small Business Journal* 14(2): 35-51.

Mason, Colin and Richard Harrison. 1999. "Editorial. Venture Capital: rationale, aims and scope." *Venture Capital* 1(1): 1-46.

Mason, Colin and Richard Harrison. 2001. "'Investment Readiness': A Critique of Government Proposals to Increase the Demand for Venture Capital." *Regional Studies* 35(7): 663-668.

Mayer, Colin, Koen Schoors, and Yishay Yafeh. 2005. "Sources of funds and investment activities of venture capital funds: evidence from Germany, Israel, Japan and the UK." *Journal of Corporate Finance* 11: 586-608.

McGlue, David. 2002. "The funding of venture capital in Europe: issues for public policy." *Venture Capital* 4(1): 45-58.

McNally, Kevin. 1997. *Corporate Venture Capital. Bridging the equity gap in the small business sector.* London: Routledge.

Murray, Gordon C. 1994. "The Second 'Equity Gap': Exit Problems for Seed and Early Stage Venture Capitalists and Their Investee Companies." *International Small Business Journal* 12(4): 59-76.

Nathusius, Klaus. 1989. "GENES: 10 Jahre Pioniertätigkeit im deutschen Venture Capital Markt." in: *International venture capital – Proceedings "fair genes" Köln 1988.* Köln: Deutscher Wirtschaftsdienst, pp. 11-25.

Neher, Darwin V. 1999. "Staged Financing: An Agency Perspective." *Review of Economic Studies* 66(2): 255-274.

Nevermann, Helga and Dieter Falk. 1986. *Venture Capital. Ein betriebswirtschaftlicher und steuerlicher Vergleich zwischen den USA und der Bundesrepublik Deutschland.* Baden-Baden: Nomos.

Noone, Charles M. and Stanley M. Rubel. 1970. *SBICs: Pioneers in Organized Venture Capital.* Chicago: Capital Publishing.

NVCA. 2003 and earlier (yearly). *National Venture Capital Association Yearbook.* Prepared by Thomson Financial/Venture Economics. Arlington: National Venture Capital Association.

OECD. 1996. *Venture Capital and Innovation.* Paris: OECD.

OECD. 1997. *Government Venture Capital for Technology-based Firms.* Paris: OECD.

Øksendal, Bertil. 1985. *Stochastic Differential Equations.* Berlin: Springer.

Paffenholz, Guido. 2004. *Exitmanagement. Desinvestitionen von Beteiligungsgesellschaften.* Lohmar: Josef Eul.

Poterba, James M. 1989. "Venture Capital and Capital Gains Taxation." NBER Working Paper No. 2832, July.

Rock, Edward B. 2001. "Greenhorns, Yankees and Cosmopolitans: Venture Capital, IPOs, Foreign Firms and U.S. Markets." Research Paper No. 01-07, Institute for Law and Economics, University of Pennsylvania Law School, February.

Roling, Jörg. 2001. *Venture Capital und Innovation. Theoretische Zusammenhänge, empirische Befunde und wirtschaftspolitische Implikationen.* Lohmar: Josef Eul.

Romer, Paul M. 1986. "Increasing Returns and Long-Run Growth." *Journal of Political Economy* 94: 1002-1037.

Romer, Paul M. 1990. "Endogenous Technological Change." *Journal of Political Economy* 98: S71-S102.

Romer, Paul M. 1994. "The Origins of Endogenous Growth." *Journal of Economic Perspectives* 8 (Winter): 3-22.

Romer, Paul M. 2000. "Should the Government Subsidize Supply or Demand in the Market for Scientists and Engineers?" NBER Working Paper No. 7723, June.

Rosen, Harvey S. 1999. *Public Finance.* 5th ed., Boston, MA: McGraw-Hill.

Rosen, Harvey S. 2005. "Entrepreneurship and Taxation: Empirical Evidence." in: Kanniainen, Vesa and Christian Keuschnigg. eds. *Venture Capital, Entrepreneurship, and Public Policy.* CESifo Seminar Series. Cambridge, MA: MIT Press, pp. 251-279.

Sahlman, William A. 1990. "The structure and governance of venture-capital organizations." *Journal of Financial Economics* 27: 473-524.

Schefczyk, Michael. 1998. *Erfolgsstrategien deutscher Venture Capital-Gesellschaften.* Stuttgart: Schaeffer-Poeschel.

Schmidt, Reinhard E. 1988. "Venture Capital in Deutschland - ein Problem der Qualität?" *Die Bank* 4/88: 184-188.

Schumpeter, Joseph. 1934[1912]. *The Theory of Economic Development.* Cambridge, MA: Harvard University Press. [originally published in German as *Theorie der wirtschaftlichen Entwicklung*, Leipzig 1912]

Schumpeter, Joseph. 1942. *Capitalism, Socialism, and Democracy.* New York: Harper.

Segerstrom, Paul S. 1998. "Endogenous Growth Without Scale Effects." *American Economic Review* 88(5): 1290-1310.

Shepherd, Dean A. and Andrew Zacharakis. 2001. "Speed to Initial Public Offering of VC-Backed Companies." *Entrepreneurship Theory and Practice*, Spring: 59-69.

Shinal, John. 2003. "UC ordered to reveal details of investments. Ruling on venture capital funds could cost university hundreds of millions in returns." *San Francisco Chronicle*, 29 August, page A.1.

Smith, Michael D. 2001. "A Second Look at the Secondary Private Equity Market." *Journal of Private Equity* 5(1): 55-65.

Sohl, Jeffrey E. 2003. "The U.S. Angel and Venture Capital Market: Recent Trends and Developments." *Journal of Private Equity*, Spring: 7-17.

Steier, Lloyd and Royston Greenwood. 2000. "Entrepreneurship and the Evolution of Angel Financial Networks." *Organization Studies* 21(1): 163-192.

Stiglitz, Joseph E. and Andrew Weiss. 1981. "Credit Rationing in Markets with Imperfect Information." *American Economic Review* 71(3): 393-410.

Stoehr, Achim A. 1976. "Wagnisfinanzierung." *Zeitschrift für das gesamte Kreditwesen* 8: 311-316.

Sykes, Hollister B. 1990. "Corporate Venture Capital: Strategies for Success." *Journal of Business Venturing* 5: 37-47.

Ueda, Masako. 2002. "Does Innovation Spur Venture Capital?" Working paper, University of Wisconson – Madison.

Ueda, Masako. (undated). "Banks versus Venture Capital: Project Evaluation, Screening, and Expropriation." Working paper, University of Wisconsin – Madison.

van Osnabrugge, Mark and Robert J. Robinson. 2001. "The influence of a venture capitalist's source of funds." *Venture Capital* 3(1): 25-39.

Wallsten, Scott J. 2000. "The effects of government-industry R&D programs on private R&D: the case of the Small Business Innovation Research program." *RAND Journal of Economics* 31(1): 82-100.

Wang, Clement K., Kangmao Wang, and Qing Lu. 2003. "Effects of venture capitalists' participation in listed companies." *Journal of Banking & Finance* 27: 2015-2034.

Wang, Susheng and Hailan Zhou. 2004. "Staged financing in venture capital: moral hazard and risks." *Journal of Corporate Finance* 10(1): 131-155.

Watrin, Christoph and Sebastian Gocksch. 2002. "Problembereiche der Besteuerung inländischer Private Equity-Fonds." *Der Betrieb*, Heft 7 (15.02.2002): 341-345.

Wirtschaftswoche. 1983. "Deutscher Venture-Capital-Markt: Ehrgeizige Startversuche." *Wirtschaftswoche* 43, October 21: 144-149.

Wright, Mike and Ken Robbie. 1998. "Venture Capital and Private Equity: A Review and Synthesis." *Journal of Business Finance & Accounting* 25(5)&(6): 521-570.

Wupperfeld, Udo. 1996. *Management und Rahmenbedingungen von Beteiligungsgesellschaften auf dem deutschen Seed-Capital-Markt: Empirische Untersuchung.* Frankfurt am Main: Peter Lang.

Young, Alwyn. 1998. "Growth without Scale Effects." *Journal of Political Economy* 106(1): 41-63.

Zemke, Ingo. 1995. *Die Unternehmensverfassung von Beteiligungskapital-Gesellschaften. Analyse des institutionellen Designs deutscher Venture Capital-Gesellschaften.* Wiesbaden: Deutscher Universitäts-Verlag.

Zider, Bob. 1998. "How Venture Capital Works." *Harvard Business Review*, November-December: 131-139.

Züchner, Patrick. 2003. "Overhang of Funds: Ursachen, Reaktionen, Folgen." *Dortmunder Diskussionsbeiträge zur Wirtschaftspolitik*, Working paper Nr. 123, University Dortmund, August.

MIX
Papier aus verantwortungsvollen Quellen
Paper from responsible sources
FSC® C105338

If you have any concerns about our products,
you can contact us on
ProductSafety@springernature.com

In case Publisher is established outside the EU,
the EU authorized representative is:
Springer Nature Customer Service Center GmbH
Europaplatz 3, 69115 Heidelberg, Germany

Printed by Libri Plureos GmbH
in Hamburg, Germany